Breaking the Silence

Breaking the Silence

*French Women's Voices
from the Ghetto*

Fadela Amara

With Sylvia Zappi

Translated with an Introduction
by Helen Harden Chenut

Originally published in France as
Ni Putes Ni Soumises (Neither Whore Nor Submissive)

UNIVERSITY OF CALIFORNIA PRESS

Berkeley   Los Angeles   London

University of California Press, one of the most distinguished university presses in the United States, enriches lives around the world by advancing scholarship in the humanities, social sciences, and natural sciences. Its activities are supported by the UC Press Foundation and by philanthropic contributions from individuals and institutions. For more information, visit www.ucpress.edu.

University of California Press
Berkeley and Los Angeles, California

University of California Press, Ltd.
London, England

Originally published in French as *Ni putes ni soumises,*
© Éditions La Découverte, Paris, France, 2003, 2004.

Library of Congress Cataloging-in-Publication Data

Amara, Fadela.
    [Ni putes ni soumises. English]
    Breaking the silence : French women's voices from the ghetto / Fadela Amara with Sylvia Zappi ; translated with an introduction by Helen Harden Chenut.
        p.   cm.
    Originally published : Ni putes ni soumises. Paris : Découverte, 2003.
    Includes bibliographical references and index.
    ISBN 0-520-24620-9 (cloth : alk. paper) — ISBN 0-520-24621-7 (pbk. : alk. paper)
    1. Sex discrimination against women—France.   2. Muslim women—France—Social conditions.   3. Suburban life—France.   4. Civil rights demonstrations—France—Paris—History—21st century.   I. Zappi, Sylvia.   II. Title.
HQ1237.5.F8A4313   2006
323.3'4'0882970944—dc22   2005023246

Manufactured in the United States of America

15   14   13   12   11   10   09   08   07   06
10 9 8 7 6 5 4 3 2 1

This book is printed on New Leaf EcoBook 60, containing 60% post-consumer waste, processed chlorine free; 30% de-inked recycled fiber, elemental chlorine free; and 10% FSC-certified virgin fiber, totally chlorine free. EcoBook 60 is acid-free and meets the minimum requirements of ANSI/ASTM D5634–01 (*Permanence of Paper*).

CONTENTS

TRANSLATOR'S INTRODUCTION

As the reader will discover, Fadela Amara is a human rights activist with both a personal and a collective voice. As a second-generation French citizen born of Algerian immigrant parents, she maps her individual path to integration in postcolonial French society. She also speaks for a group, the children of North African immigrants in contemporary France, a nation now confronted by major ethnic tensions and the emergence of Muslim fundamentalism. France has the largest Muslim population in Europe, largely drawn from former colonies on the North African coast. Major French cities face problems of unemployment, racial discrimination, and violence centered in ghetto-like suburban communities where Muslims form a large majority. Most recently, the French government's efforts to deal with visible signs of a Muslim presence in French society by banning headscarves and other religious symbols in secular public schools have proved highly controversial and divisive.[1] The law directed against wearing religious symbols in public schools has provoked, in fact, a nationwide debate over the relation between religion and politics in society and revealed social tensions at many levels.

Amara identifies herself as a girl born in the province of Auvergne in central France, one of ten children in a strongly patriarchal Algerian working-class family. She makes a persuasive case that, despite latent anti-Arab discrimination, young women of her second generation felt more socially integrated than those of the present third generation. In fact, she argues, deteriorating living conditions in suburban immigrant communities and the rise of violence and of Islamic fundamentalism have made those young people second-class citizens. In this context Amara founded a movement called Ni Putes Ni Soumises—roughly translated as Neither Whore Nor Submissive—aimed at shattering the law of silence within the Muslim community concerning violence perpetrated against women by a minority of young men who assumed the role of morals police and guardians of their family's honor. The movement's title and banner were created in March 2002 in the founding appeal (see its text in appendix 1). Amara explains the deliberately provocative slogan as a reply, first, to macho Muslim men who constantly refer to young women as "all whores except my mother"; and as a challenge, second, to those French observers "who believe that if we are oppressed, it's because we refuse to rebel."[2] Behind this bold title is the central goal of freeing Muslim women to speak out against rising male violence and oppression. But, as the subsequent manifesto demonstrates (appendix 2), the movement also has a broad agenda for social change within the suburban immigrant community, and a particular set of demands concerning young Muslim women. The demands cite the urgent need to ensure women's freedom of movement within and outside their communities, their physical security in mixed-sex company, and the possibility of voicing their vision of future gender equality as citizens of the French Republic. Affirming their voice, speaking for themselves, breaking taboos are all at the heart of a movement that finds itself in the midst of an intense debate. While many young Muslim women taking part in this movement do not readily identify themselves as feminists, their movement shares many of contemporary feminism's goals. It is self-styled as secular, pluralistic, and inclusive of men. To this end the movement's manifesto opens with the recognition that racial discrimination and unemployment of North African men in the housing projects cause social and economic marginalization and contribute to the injustice that has affected the community as a whole. Nevertheless, the movement and its leader must counter charges that their actions and high media coverage further stigmatize Muslim men of their own community. Other critics note that the suburban violence they describe is a much more pervasive phenomenon that affects populations of other nationalities, religions, and races.[3]

Amara's movement thus addresses a host of broader and interconnected issues: the history of North African immigration within France's colonial past; the difficult integration of these populations—subject to high unemployment—within a society commonly viewed as supportive of human rights; the degradation of the suburbs that increasingly marginalizes immigrant communities, leaving them vulnerable to violence, delinquency, and predatory behavior by a minority of young men against young women. These socioeconomic issues of marginalization are further complicated by the irruption of Islamic fundamentalism into the suburbs and the subsequent policing of young women's behavior to conform to Islamic dress codes that impose headscarves for women in public. The association Ni Putes Ni Soumises reached out to the Muslim and immigrant community by organizing a march through twenty-three French cities and towns to collect testimony from other Muslim women, a march that aimed squarely at breaking the silence within their communities concerning these very issues. The leaders arrived in Paris on 8 March 2003, bringing together more than thirty thousand supporters, primarily from the suburbs, to call the government's attention to their cause. The government was forced to react to their demands for a policy of deliberate rehabilitation of the suburban landscape and for the funding of special social services for young women that the immigrant communities themselves would run.

Written as a follow-up to the march, this book created a sensation within France as a work of politically committed testimony. It was taken seriously as a "political project," winning an annual award from the French National Assembly as the best political book of 2003. Subsequent prizes noted the author's contribution toward the respect of human rights and secularism. Nevertheless, reactions to Amara's book and to her activism within the Muslim community reveal a number of conflicting social tensions that are linked, as we shall see, to France's colonial past, to France's policies regarding immigration, to the rise of fundamentalism within French Islam, and to women's rights.

THE COLONIAL PAST

France is home to some five million Muslims representing nearly 10 percent of its total population.[4] Perhaps more significant in the current political context is the fact that Islam is now the second largest religion in France after Catholicism. An overwhelming majority of Muslims come from France's overseas colonies on the northern coast of Africa (Algeria, Tunisia, and Morocco; collectively, the Maghreb). Overseas expansion into Algeria had begun before the French Revolution of 1789 with coastal trading posts, and in 1830 France conquered Algiers ostensibly to settle a financial and diplomatic incident. During the following forty years France extended its rule over the coastal areas and into the Saharan interior through a series of military campaigns that were clearly designed as part of a colonial enterprise. By expropriating lands, suppressing resistance from nationalist leaders and chieftains, uprooting and displacing tribes, and encouraging settlers from southern European countries across the Mediterranean, France established Algeria as the main site of its colonial economic interests. Subsequent republican governments envisaged a policy of integrating the European populations of Algeria into metropolitan France, even offering them representation within the National Assembly in Paris. In fact, a law passed in 1889 confirmed the existing racial hierarchy by extending French citizenship to settlers of European origin, half of whom were French, while Muslims and Jews in Algeria remained subject to Islamic law.[5]

By 1880 the Ottoman Turks' control over North Africa had markedly declined, and France moved to extend its interests and trading privileges in Tunisia. As the European powers met in Berlin to consider the future of the Ottoman Empire, France positioned itself to take control of Tunisia and in 1881, after an incident on the Algerian border, forced the ruling bey in Tunis to grant France a protectorate over his country. Morocco's status, by contrast, was more complex, since it was recognized by several European powers as an independent country and important trading partner. By the late nineteenth century, however, Morocco faced financial problems and increased pressure from Britain, France, and Spain for preferential trading concessions. The ensuing diplomatic scramble among the Europeans to colonize the remaining portions of North Africa allowed an ambitious French officer, Hubert Lyautey, to invade western Morocco in 1903 and strengthen France's position for a takeover. Serious diplomatic crises and military standoffs in 1906 and again in 1911 also involved Germany, whose imperial ambitions in Morocco clashed with those of France. A treaty signed in 1912 with the ruling sultan, narrowly averting war, granted France a protectorate over Morocco. But armed resistance to French conquest and occupation continued for many years.

French colonial domination over Algeria under direct rule was to have far more long-lasting consequences than those resulting from the protectorate administration in neighboring Tunisia and Morocco. For Algerian peasants colonization meant the expropriation of their land and the destruction of their traditional economy and society. Faced with poverty, many of these landless peasants found an option for survival in emigration to Algerian cities or to France itself.[6] During and after World War I Algerian laborers were offered special residence papers and jobs to help rebuild France and offset the loss of manpower. But these immigrant workers were given no recognition by French authorities that they would be, or could potentially be, assimilated into society on equal terms with native French citizens. They were widely perceived as a foreign community whose values and religious beliefs were at odds with secular French society. Moreover, during the 1920s and 1930s colonial officials encouraged close political surveillance of Algerians in France as a means of controlling outbreaks of nationalist sentiment within that community.[7]

After 1947 the expansion of the French economy and a greater freedom of movement between the two countries markedly increased Algerian immigration. The irony was that Muslim Algerians (but not Tunisians or Moroccans) now had the possibility of becoming French citizens, since Algeria was considered an integral part of metropolitan France.[8] Those Algerian workers who had stable employment were authorized to have their families join them according to a policy of *regroupement familial* (family reunification). Despite the contradictions of feeling torn between two countries, many Algerians in France were convinced that exile from home was temporary. The outbreak of the Algerian War for independence in 1954 radically changed the situation. French army efforts to relocate and pacify the Algerian countryside disrupted rural life, encouraging larger numbers of Algerian Muslims to emigrate to France. Two rival independence movements, the Front de libération nationale and the Mouvement national algérien, sought funding and support from Muslims in France and Algeria alike. In retaliation, French authorities closely policed and repressed any demonstrations by immigrants in favor of independence.[9]

The Algerian War for independence represented a trauma for both sides. The French army, humiliated by military defeat in Indochina in 1954, was determined to put down the rebellion in Algeria, and it drew on the support of the French colonists, many of whom had lived there for generations. The brutal conflict opposed a rebel clandestine guerilla force against an army dominated by young conscripts led by professional officers seasoned in colonial combat.[10] The French army displaced entire rural populations in order to pacify and control the country. But the conflict also brought metropolitan France to the verge of civil war. When a rebellion led by extremist French generals and colonists defied the Paris government in May 1958, the retired general and political leader Charles de Gaulle was recalled and ultimately oversaw the demise of the French Fourth Republic. Violence continued with bomb attacks in the heart of Paris, before de Gaulle finally managed to resolve the Algerian crisis. A new French constitution for the Fifth Republic, approved by popular referendum, reinforced his power for tough negotiations that subsequently led to peace talks with the Algerian liberation leaders.

The Evian accords in 1962 marked the bitter end of the war and the recognition by France of Algerian independence. Included in the agreements were a number of guarantees for both sides: the safeguard of French property in Algeria, and French citizenship for Algerians born in what was officially the French department of Algeria before independence, on the condition that they apply for naturalization. Yet the settlement unleashed new waves of emigration: colonists returning to France, Algerians who had fought with the French army (known as *harkis*), and civilian Algerian emigrants who opted for life in France—some 180,000 in 1962 and 262,000 in 1963.[11] But issues of citizenship, particularly the exercise of political rights, were complex in the aftermath of the war. Many Algerian Muslims already in France elected to stay, as Fadela Amara's testimony confirms in the case of her parents. She speaks proudly of her own French citizenship, while explaining that her family members represent "a puzzle of nationalities." Citizenship rights for

Algerian Muslims living in France are but one of the troubled legacies of the Algerian War.

NORTH AFRICAN IMMIGRANTS IN FRANCE

As we have seen, Algerian migration to France began before 1914, as a direct consequence of colonization and in response to a decline in the French labor force. Many of the first immigrants came from the Berber region of Kabylia, as "guest workers" in a rotating exchange that allowed them to return home. However, during the immediate post-1945 years of prosperity, North Africans arrived in France in far greater numbers to meet the needs of an expanding labor market. In contrast to those immigrants of European origin who arrived during the late nineteenth-century industrialization and in the interwar years—from Italy, Belgium, and Poland—and who integrated relatively rapidly into the French Third Republic, North Africans had a difficult experience. They were provided with poor housing in transit centers and were assigned the low-skilled and often unhealthy work that others refused to do. During periods of economic recession they were often the first workers to be laid off. Within French society they encountered racial discrimination, social marginalization, and, in the case of the Algerians, political suspicion after the war began. A large number of these first-generation immigrants nurtured the dream of eventually returning to their home country. But overall the North African immigrants remained in France, growing from 28.2 percent of the total foreign population in 1975 to 39.1 percent in 1990.[12] In 1973 the Algerian government suspended worker emigration to France in response to the growing number of racist attacks against its nationals, and the following year France did the same in the wake of increasing unemployment and economic recession. These measures ended nearly a century of Algerian emigration and exchange.

In the interim, the French government had set up social services for Algerians to promote their integration as immigrant workers. French welfare state provisions were extended to them as the government sought to win the Algerian immigrants' loyalty away from the nationalist movement. The government also delegated private Catholic organizations with the role of providing direct services to Algerians. Human rights and solidarity organizations (such as the Mouvement contre le racisme et pour l'amitié entre les peuples), together with leftist political parties and labor unions, also sought to improve the overall living and working conditions of immigrant workers. A public organization (the Fonds d'action sociale), created in 1958 to allocate funds for services and for surveillance of Algerians, later provided extended social services and subsidies to immigrant communities. Such reform and welfare measures were generally effective until the economic recession of the 1980s.

During this decade Jean-Marie Le Pen led the Front national (FN), his Far Right political party, in politicizing the issue of immigration. Le Pen branded North African Muslims in particular as being incapable of assimilation because of their religious and cultural differences. In spite of his openly racist and provocative rhetoric that included distortions of the historical record, Le Pen responded to voters' fears that immigration was changing the ethnic balance within their country; he managed to garner regular support from between 10 and 15 percent of voters during the 1980s. A portion of these voters came from the French working class in the industrial regions of northern and eastern France, where racial tensions were exacerbated in the 1990s by increasing unemployment and economic recession. The FN also found support in southern France among the large numbers of former French settlers in Algeria, the *pieds-noirs*, who often maintained a particular hatred of Muslims. Le Pen even scored surprisingly high in the first round of the presidential elections in 2002, although he was substantially defeated in the final round by the incumbent, Jacques Chirac.[13]

To combat the FN's electoral strength, political parties of both the traditional Right and the socialist Left were forced to define stronger policies to control the influx of illegal immigrants during their years in power after 1981. The Right resorted to chartering airplanes to return illegal immigrants to their home countries, and to cracking down on North African immigrants accused of petty crimes, sentencing them first to prison terms and then deporting them to their countries of origin. This practice, called *double peine*, was widely condemned; in many cases the individuals in question did not speak the language of the countries to which they were sent. The Socialists, in contrast, undertook a reform of the nationality code and attempted to regularize the situation of illegal immigrants through a temporary amnesty. In 1981 the Socialist government of the newly elected president, François Mitterrand, authorized immigrants to organize cultural associations, providing them with the means to obtain financial aid for cultural activities such as theater and music.

Despite these initiatives, a series of racially motivated murders and other violence against North African Muslims broke out during the early 1980s. By this time the children of North

African immigrants, the second generation, had come of age. In 1983 they organized their first protest march from Lyon to Paris—a "march for equality and against racism," known as the marche des Beurs—to denounce the racial violence and threats of expulsion that targeted them. This action was part of a larger struggle for equal rights and for recognition of their identity. In his personal account of the march, Bouzid refused several of the labels identifying his generation, including the designation as "second": "Why are Arabs the only immigrants to whom one gives a number?" he asked.[14] Indeed, many North African youth of Algerian parentage had difficulty identifying themselves as either French or Algerian for reasons that stemmed from the legacy of the Algerian War and from their sense of rejection.[15] Understandably, they aspired for better status than their parents, whose experience of humiliation and marginalization had marked the children's lives as well. Moreover, they felt rejected by the French working class, which was reluctant to integrate "immigrant" issues into the problems of a postindustrial society.

The slogan brandished by the demonstrators during the Beur March has had a long life: "première, deuxième, troisième génération: nous sommes tous des enfants d'immigrés!" (First, second, third generation: we are all children of immigrants!). It asked for public recognition of immigration's impact on twentieth-century France—despite what one historian has termed "collective amnesia" with respect to its history—and claimed the demonstrators' place within it.[16] The youths who dominated this first march identified themselves as Beurs. They were North African males between the ages of about fifteen and thirty, who inhabited the suburbs of Paris and other major cities; the female version of *beur*, less frequently used and carrying a more positive connotation, is *beurette*.[17] Both terms originated in the slang known as Verlan, a reverse language (or *l'envers*) used in both white and ethnic suburban communities. When the media identified suburban youths of ethnic origins accused of delinquency and violence as Beur, young North Africans switched to Rebeus, a Verlan variant on it. But the Beur movement's style of cultural expression and political mobilization for integration, largely based on difference, has left a collective history in music, theater, and television.

Members of this second generation "accepted French egalitarian values and aspirations," and their demand for recognition is a sign of their "successful assimilation of mainstream French values and cultural practices." In this sense their mobilization for collective political action reveals that they found the "fear of deportation, substandard housing, school tracking, police harassment, and an often-biased justice system particularly unacceptable."[18] In fact, Fadela Amara cites incidents of police injustice in her Algerian community of suburban Clermont-Ferrand during her youth that marked the first stirrings of her own conscience as a human rights activist. The march drew considerable media attention and support from French public opinion and political authorities. Its success can be attributed to support from "minority immigrant associations, solidarity movements, and the political left."[19] Certainly its most tangible result was the granting by the Mitterand government of ten-year residence and work permits to foreign workers. Promises were also made to pursue serious punishment for racially motivated crimes and to consider the possibility of giving foreign residents the right to vote in local elections.

Subsequent protest marches and demonstrations that were organized by different, and often rival, immigrant associations, such as Convergence 1984 and France Plus, had limited success because their leaders were divided over strategies. They were forced either to seek broad alliances with solidarity groups and political parties to achieve their goals and maintain financial support or to claim the autonomy and integrity of their movement, free from manipulation by outside political forces, at the risk of losing members and funding. One of the most successful and popular associations to emerge at this time was SOS Racisme, led by a charismatic and media-savvy leader named Harlem Désir. The association flourished in the mid-1980s under the patronage of the Socialist Party and its leaders. By focusing its platform primarily on combating racism and on promoting solidarity among all racial groups, the movement culled national support from the student generation and other groups concerned with inequality and injustice across French society through a variety of highly publicized fundraising events. Its popularity as a multicultural, broad-based organization was also sustained by a clever iconic badge, a bright yellow hand with the phrase "Touche pas à mon pote" (Hands off my buddy). While SOS Racisme continued its operations through the 1980s thanks to Socialist Party funding, a split developed between its leadership and its supporters: members charged that many of its militant leaders had been promoted out of the suburbs and into the *beurgeoisie.* Whether or not SOS Racisme had indeed been co-opted by outside political forces, many North African youths felt that their association's leaders had turned their backs on their community and had failed to obtain significant changes or tangible results.[20] This negative legacy and a worsening economic situation in France in the late 1980s turned immigrant youth inward to their own communities. As ethnic minority associations declined, Islamic fundamentalist groups moved into the vacuum, establishing bases in the suburbs and offering young North African men in particular a seemingly more meaningful identity.

THE CREATION OF NI PUTES NI SOUMISES

Fadela Amara traces her militant roots to participation in SOS Racisme, an organization that she felt was more inclusive in its concerns than previous ones, open to ethnic diversity, to women's issues, and to organization at the local community level where she worked. There in her own community she saw the increasing degradation of gender relations into violence and the socioeconomic problems that underpinned this process, which she analyzes in this book. She founded a commission to focus on women's issues and inaugurated a training workshop on the history of Western feminism for her colleagues at the Fédération nationale des maisons des potes (national federation of solidarity houses).[21] She then organized a national meeting in early 2002, open only to women from its local chapters, a meeting called the Estates General (or general assembly) of Neighborhood Women. It aimed at opening a dialogue across generations within immigrant communities about issues of central concern to women. This meeting led to the drafting of the manifesto of Ni Putes Ni Soumises and the creation of the group whose goal was to shatter the law of silence about violence against young Muslim women in French immigrant communities.

But what prompted Fadela to act was the murder of Sohane Benziane. In October 2002 this eighteen-year-old Muslim woman was set on fire for her rebellious behavior by a local gang leader in Vitry-sur-Seine, a suburb of southern Paris.[22] She was a victim of the kind of hypermasculine behavior to enforce Islamist codes of sexual behavior that Amara denounces. Another young woman, Samira Bellil, had courageously spoken out in a book titled *Dans l'enfer des tournantes*, denouncing the violent gang rapes of young Muslim women for rebelling against the Islamic dress codes and gender-based behavior imposed by their older brothers. Together with Samira and others Fadela organized a five-week march in spring 2003, encouraging women and men in Muslim communities to voice their concerns during public debates in twenty-three cities and suburbs in France (see map). This "tour de France" finished in Paris on 8 March 2003 to mark International Women's Day.

The positive reactions in the Parisian and the provincial press confirmed the march's public success. A meeting with the prime minister produced promises of support for a number of demands listed on the group's collective appeal, raising cautious optimism that their efforts might obtain concrete results. However, Amara also notes the criticism the association faced from several organized groups who came to disturb the public meetings and debates during the march. The most virulent opposition came from Islamic fundamentalists in the audience who accused her of carrying out a campaign to denigrate Islam and stigmatize Muslim men. Her defense of secular values, they charged, was part of a neocolonialist project of "assimilation," evidence that she and her group were being used by political forces within the government. Other critics from within the North African community,

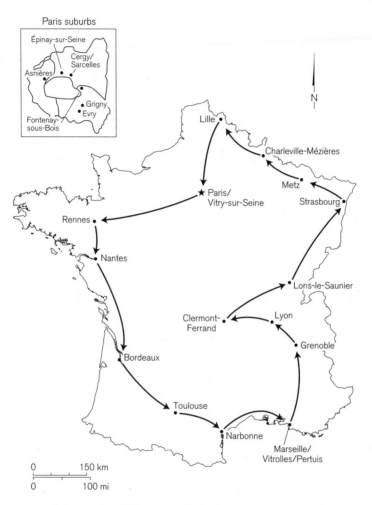

Paris suburbs

Épinay-sur-Seine

Cergy/
Sarcelles

Asnières

Grigny
Evry

Fontenay-
sous-Bois

N

Lille

Charleville-Mézières

Metz

★ Paris/
Vitry-sur-Seine

Strasbourg

Rennes

Nantes

Lons-le-Saunier

Clermont-
Ferrand

Lyon

Grenoble

Bordeaux

Toulouse

Narbonne

Marseille/
Vitrolles/Pertuis

0   150 km

0   100 mi

Route of the march, 1 February to 8 March, 2003.

including men who had participated in the Beur March, argued that her movement would be co-opted by political parties and by feminist organizations. They charged that it would fail to obtain substantive gains, much as had occurred in the movements of the 1980s.[23] The negative legacy of the male-led Beur movements was intensely felt within the community. More subtle criticism of Amara's positions and the association's action was leveled by French leftist intellectuals, who, as she explains in her postscript, support the "right to difference" voiced by militant Muslim groups in defense of wearing headscarves, now banned in French public schools. The dissonance of such attacks reveals a crisis within France over values and institutions such as *laïcité*, or secularism, and the historic role of the public school system in transmitting republican values of liberty, equality, and fraternity. Many French officials, politicians, and citizens are asking whether such religious symbols as headscarves represent a serious challenge to the French state itself.

LAÏCITÉ AND HEADSCARVES

Fadela Amara's analysis of how Islamic fundamentalists moved into suburban neighborhoods and how they came to have the influence they did confirms what we know about the socioeconomic factors contributing to the resurgence of Islam among young people in many other parts of the world. She describes a situation of rising unemployment, racial discrimination, social exclusion, and neglect that breeds widespread feelings of injustice and revolt. For North African men in particular, Islamic fundamentalism (or Islamism, as it is also called) can provide a recognized identity, a new ethic and a message of promise for the future. But according to Amara, fundamentalism's message for young women is one of regression toward patriarchy, submission imposed sometimes by violence, and seclusion within their community. In her view, a headscarf represents the most visible symbol of what she terms "obscurantist" minority pressure. As she argues in chapter 6, "The headscarf is not simply a religious matter. Remember that it is first of all a means of oppression, of alienation, of discrimination, an instrument of power over women used by men."

To counter the influence of this fundamentalist version of Islam, Amara believes, the government must negotiate and act. The key to North African integration must begin with a commitment to redress social and economic injustices faced by Muslim citizens, particularly by rehabilitating the public housing projects in which they live. At the same time, the Muslim community itself must respect the secular republican tradition within the public school system. Despite her own difficulties at school, Amara considers this secular space to be one of the strongest means of integration into French society. Historically this has indeed proven to be the case. The gradual secularization of French society began with the Enlightenment and the French Revolution. Only after a protracted struggle over the course of the nineteenth century was a more permanent separation of church and state enacted into law in 1905.[24] Expressions of religious convictions and cultural differences are in principle considered private matters and are to be discouraged in all public institutions, including the school system. Yet tensions have existed between religion and politics in the public sphere, requiring continued negotiation and compromise. In today's ideological climate of resurgent Islam, there is perhaps a need to define what *laïcité* involves and what role the French school system might play in reducing social tensions.[25] Because many French citizens feel that their historic social values and institutions are under attack by militant Islam, they strongly defend the principle of a secular civil society. The defense of secularism as a civic norm, in fact, crosses social class and political lines. But some critics question whether the French are not attempting to enshrine this secular principle into a notion of exceptionalism, rather than accepting to negotiate a place for Islam as the second religion of France.[26]

The first appearance of Islamic headscarves in public schools was in 1989 in Creil, a suburb of Paris, among a very small number of students in middle school. The girls were sent home on probation for refusing to remove them in the classroom, while the minister of education at the time, Lionel Jospin, asked for guidelines from the Conseil d'Etat (council of state), the highest administrative court in France. The council ruled that wearing headscarves in school was compatible with secularism and thus legal, provided that it did not intrude on others' rights to religious freedom or in any way entail proselytism. The council also advised negotiation in schools on a case-by-case basis. But ten years later the wearing of headscarves was rapidly becoming a much more widespread phenomenon. Many French citizens now perceived it as a sign of provocation. By 2003 the increasing incidence of girls in headscarves served to focus anxieties on a whole range of social and political problems: fears of insecurity in North African neighborhoods, such as Fadela Amara describes, troubling French and immigrant communities alike; fears of terrorism from within militant Islamic fundamentalism; a resurgence of memories of France's colonial past, particularly the Algerian war;[27] fears of the loss of "French identity" in the process of integrating the Muslim community; and finally, the persistence of Jean-Marie Le Pen's xenophobic attacks on immigration, provoking racial hatred and anti-Semitism. In a sense, immigrants had become the scapegoats for a host of social and economic ills. Young Muslim women in headscarves embodied a racialized "other," visible evidence of all that was foreign in contemporary French society.

Within this climate of social tension President Jacques Chirac created a special commission on secularism, headed by Bernard Stasi and including religious leaders, teachers, politicians, historians, and sociologists. The commission was charged with reviewing the existing laws concerning the principle of secularism in the country and recommending any necessary clarification and amendment. In 2004 the commission drew up a report that offered some twenty-five proposals. Several of these proposals recommended urban renewal projects to eliminate the worst social and economic conditions faced by Muslim immigrants. Chirac, however, decided to act immediately on only one, the most symbolic of the commission's recommendations, the ban in all public schools of the wearing of ostentatious religious symbols of all kinds—including headscarves, skullcaps, large crosses, and turbans. The ban was signed into law in March 2004 in time to prepare for its application when schools reopened in September. Although the law concerned all religious symbols, it soon became publicly known as the "anti-headscarf law," a designation that seemed to stigmatize Islam and risked exposing young Muslim women to exclusion from public schools. It thus did little to calm the debate or bridge divisions within the country over the issue. In many respects the ban was viewed as a political maneuver, as a way for the center-right government to silence criticism from the extreme right wing that the government was not acting against forces intent on destabilizing the republic.[28]

Mixed reactions to the ban within the Muslim community itself revealed divisions that reflect the pluralism of French Islam and the rivalries between various national and ethnic groups. France has only recently established a representative central organization of Muslim clerics with authority to speak for the Muslim community, called the Conseil français du culte musulman (French council of Muslim religion). Within this umbrella group are several rival associations representing different religious and political tendencies. The latest elections (2005) to this council strengthened the position of the former president, Dalil Boubakeur, a moderate and the rector of the grand mosque in Paris. The second and largest component, the Fédération nationale des musulmans de France, is dominated by practicing Muslims of Moroccan origins. A third powerful group, the Union des organisations islamiques de France (union of French Islamic organizations), led by Fouad Alaoui, represents a more militant fundamentalist group.[29] Alaoui's group opposes the headscarf ban and in 1989 undertook to defend in court the Muslim women students who had been suspended. The group was preparing to renew its campaign in autumn 2004 as the law banning religious symbols went into effect but suspended its plan when two French journalists, both specialists on the Islamic world, were kidnapped in Iraq. The hostage takers issued an ultimatum to the French government to revoke the law banning headscarves in schools.

It is difficult to judge to what extent the headscarf ban has divided the French Muslim community. Many of its members have been educated in France and are probably more secularized in attitude than the image conveyed by the media. The hostage crisis of autumn 2004 gave French Muslims the opportunity to demonstrate their solidarity with France and they did so in significant numbers by supporting the government's rejection of the terrorists' ultimatum. A representative group of French Muslim leaders even traveled to Baghdad to assist in negotiations. At the same time, those most concerned by the ban— Muslim women students—returned to school with or without headscarves and negotiated with teachers over the new regulations.[30] Only a small number were ultimately expelled during the first months the ban was in place.

Empowering the many Muslim girls in secondary schools to give voice to their demands is an essential part of the project Fadela Amara launched in Ni Putes Ni Soumises. In France's secular society wearing the headscarf conveys ambiguous meanings, both private and public, to which the media contribute by identifying the scarf with the more militant aspects of Islam today. A sociological study entitled *Le foulard et la République* (1995) explored its multiple meanings on the basis of in-depth interviews with young men and women living in suburban communities. The authors, Françoise Gaspard and Farhad Khosrokhavar, provided some interesting insights into the behavior of adolescent secondary-school girls and other young women between the ages of sixteen and twenty-five who wore headscarves. Two dominant models of behavior emerged from their study. A first group of young women was essentially compelled to wear the headscarf in order to please parents or older brothers, as a compromise between traditional family codes and modern secularized values. A second group of women self-consciously chose to wear the headscarf as an affirmation of their identity, as "being both French and Muslim, modern and *voilée*, autonomous and dressed in Islamic costume."[31] This second group was characterized, above all, by postadolescent women who were often well educated and even integrated into French culture and society. According to Gaspard and Khosrokhavar, these young women were affirming a positive individual difference to counter what they perceived as racist treatment by the French. Their intention was to "become visible" when before they had felt invisible. The authors contend that all forms of the headscarf worn by those young women interviewed were "non-political."[32] As the reader will see, Fadela Amara has her own typology of the young women who wear the headscarf in French Muslim communities, and her own opinion as to its meanings.

Françoise Gaspard, a leading militant for women's rights in France, warns against the treatment of French Islam as a homogeneous block, when in fact it includes many currents that affirm tolerance. Women's rights, she argues, are better served by not banning the headscarf. Expelling girls from French public schools deprives them of their right to education and of a path to modernity.[33] Many feminists, Gaspard among them, pointed to the contradictions within French politics and society on the issue of women's rights. An amendment to the French constitution passed in 2000 was widely debated as to whether it would effectively increase women's access to elected political office by ensuring their candidature in numbers equal to men.[34] The parity law has had little notable effect. Ségolène Royal, a popular French deputy to the National Assembly from the Socialist Party, also expressed ambivalence toward the headscarf law (though she voted for it), citing other contradictions in French society with regard to women. As just one example, she voiced her opposition to the flagrantly sexualized images of female bodies displayed on French billboards.[35]

The headscarf affair, associated with the denunciation of violence against women by Ni Putes Ni Soumises, has broken a taboo within the Muslim community against public discussions of sexuality. Fadela Amara identifies a real need for more sex education in schools, education that treats questions of desire, pleasure, and respect for one's partner. She has witnessed the suffering caused by hidden sexuality among young men and women whose families impose mandatory virginity and, in some cases, forced marriages to uphold family honor as determined by traditional community values. At stake is the right of young Muslim women to have control over their own bodies and sexuality. In fact, the debates within the Islamic community over gendered codes of behavior have revived long-standing tensions between secularism and religious belief on issues of female sexuality. Islamic religious leaders define women's chastity as the basis of communal identity within their traditional vision of a "natural" social and political order. Muslim men in France may feel threatened by the loss of social control over North African women, many of whom are drawn to modern individualistic values and forms of emancipation as a result of their public education. There is little doubt that Fadela Amara's empowering message of female emancipation and individual rights clashes overtly with fundamentalist assertions of religious and patriarchal authority. Similarly, her discussion of male homosexuality breaks another taboo by asserting that young gay men in the projects incur the same hypermasculine pressure to conform to gender and sexual norms as young women do.[36] According to Amara, they too must benefit from the respect of individual rights.

WOMEN'S RIGHTS AND HUMAN RIGHTS

Since its creation in 2003 Ni Putes Ni Soumises has grown from an ethnic minority movement to an organization of substantially greater social and political diversity, garnering widespread support. Its impact comes in part from revealing underlying social and political tensions in France today. The immediate problem facing Amara and her association is how to obtain concrete results from the French center-right government that, by agreeing in March 2003 to fund a series of emergency measures for young Muslim women, greatly raised hopes and expectations in their communities. Such measures include the creation of shelters for family runaways and victims of male violence, and the distribution of a printed guide to schools and neighborhood centers promoting respect and communication between men and women in the housing projects. The newly printed guide to respect represents the most recent result. Given the absence of any discussion in families, the guide offers young people clear guidelines on sexuality and respect for their body and that of their partner and warns against physical and psychological violence toward women and girls within the framework of French law.[37]

Amara and her co-workers have challenged the French Republic and its male leadership, using a strategy that champions republican secular values and stresses the language of universalism to militate in favor of individual rights. Women's rights are human rights, they argue, thus casting their demands for equality between men and women in terms of a broader struggle for democratic freedoms. In its International Women's Day tract of 2005, the group affirmed that the degree of women's emancipation in a given society is the best measure of democratic practice within that society.[38] In defense of this notion the leaders of Ni Putes Ni Soumises reiterate their opposition to Islamic fundamentalism and traditional practices that infringe on human rights, particularly those of women. They charge that partisans of cultural relativism are undermining women's rights by condoning archaic practices that encourage an "Islamization of the mind" and maintain male domination over women's bodies and sexuality. Fadela Amara's defense of the principle of secularism remains key to her combat against fundamentalism.

Even so, in the current political climate of identity politics, the affirmation of being both Muslim and French challenges what some observers call a "fable of primordial, continuous Frenchness." To answer this challenge the French must come up with a new model for the integration of Muslim and other immigrant populations, a model that acknowledges their identity within the French colonial past and embraces them as equal citizens in the historical narrative of the republic. Many members of the present government were political actors during the decolonization of Algeria and may find their "collective amnesia" with respect to immigration hard to overcome.[39] But Fadela Amara's message, proposing the rebuilding of the suburbs and the fostering of social and gender equality, transcends social class and political divisions and offers hope for the future.

Helen Harden Chenut
University of California–Irvine

NOTES

1. I have consistently translated the terms *voile* and *foulard* as "headscarf" to indicate the large scarf that entirely covers a woman's hair in Muslim countries.

2. Quoted in Modniss H. Abdallah, "La banlieue côté filles," *Hommes et immigration*, no. 1243 (May 2003): 101.

3. Thierry Leclère, "Violence sexiste," *Télérama*, 12 November 2004. The author cites the opinion of Christelle Hamel, an anthropologist who works on gender relations in the Maghreb immigrant community.

4. Jane Kramer, "Taking the Veil," *New Yorker*, 22 November 2004, 60.

5. Amy Lyons, "Invisible Immigrants: Algerian Families and the French Welfare State in the Era of Decolonization (1947–1974)" (Ph.D. diss., University of California–Irvine, 2004), 32–34.

6. Abdelmalek Sayad, an Algerian sociologist, asserts that after the rural insurrection of 1871, followed by French military and economic repression, "colonization, expropriation, and proletarianization" were the means with which "France traced . . . the path to [Algerian] emigration." Alain Gillette and Abdelmalek Sayad, *L'immigration algérienne en France*, 2nd ed. (Paris: Entente, 1984), 84.

7. Clifford Rosenberg, "The Colonial Politics of Health Care Provision in Interwar Paris," *French Historical Studies* 27 (Summer 2004): 637–68.

8. The law of 1947 governing French Algeria created a separate process for Muslim Algerians to acquire French nationality, a process of naturalization that required renouncing their personal status under Islamic law. In fact, this law "offered Muslim Algerians citizenship within prescribed limits . . . and claimed to offer equality while maintaining a thinly veiled racial hierarchy among citizens." Lyons, "Invisible Immigrants," 46–48.

9. The brutal repression by the Paris police of a demonstration involving 30,000 to 40,000 Algerians on 17 October 1961 resulted in the murder of an unconfirmed number of Algerians and remains part of the painful history of the Algerian War.

10. *The Battle of Algiers*, a 1966 film by Gilles Pontecorvo with some archival footage, represents the brutality of the war against French

colonialism as viewed from Algiers. It shows Algerian women taking an important role in the resistance to French occupation, notably by unveiling and carrying bombs into the European part of Algiers. Though initially banned by the French government, the film won an Academy award.

11. Gillette and Sayad, *Immigration algérienne*, 90–97; Philippe Bernard, "Les beurs, légataires du 'grand bug,'" *Le Monde*, 10 October 2004. The *harkis* received long-denied official recognition and compensation in a controversial French law passed in February 2005.

12. Miriam Feldblum, *Reconstructing Citizenship: The Politics of Nationality Reform and Immigration in Contemporary France* (Albany: SUNY Press, 1999): 21–22. In 1990 Algerians accounted for 17.2 percent of the foreign population. Their decreasing numbers reflect the increasing numbers of Algerians who obtained naturalization in France.

13. Le Pen's record as an army veteran of the Algerian War and his proposals to repatriate postcolonial minorities earned him the electoral support of former French settlers in Algeria.

14. Bouzid, *La Marche* (Paris: Sinbad, 1984), 14, as cited in Gillette and Sayad, *Immigration algérienne*, 239. See also the comments of Feldblum, *Reconstructing Citizenship*, 24, on the label of second generation as meaning non-French.

15. Gillette and Sayad, *Immigration algérienne*, 232–47. *Beur* means "Arab" in Verlan (discussed below) and originally designated this second generation.

16. Gérard Noiriel, *The French Melting Pot* (Minneapolis: University of Minnesota Press, 1996), xii.

17. Richard L. Derderian, *North Africans in Contemporary France: Becoming Visible* (New York: Palgrave Macmillan, 2004), 12–13. See also Catherine Wihtol de Wenden and Rémy Leveau, *La Beurgeoisie: les trois âges de la vie associative issue de l'immigration* (Paris: CNRS Editions, 2001), 43–44, which stresses the cultural style and modes of expression in rap music, theater, literature, and radio associated with the Beur movement in urban France. The movement also advocated a form of militancy and mobilization for integration.

18. Derderian, *North Africans*, 25. His source here is Didier Lapeyronnie, "Assimilation, mobilization et action collective chez les jeunes de la seconde génération de l'immigration Maghrébine," *Revue*

française de sociologie 28 (1987): 287–317. See also a similar analysis by de Wenden and Leveau in *Beurgeoisie*, 44–45.

19. Derderian, *North Africans*, 31–32.

20. Ibid., 37.

21. The term *pote* means "buddy" or "pal." I translated the association's title to render its mission: to create solidarity within immigrant communities and to obtain improvements in living conditions from local administrative officials.

22. In chapter 7 Amara discusses the crime.

23. Abdallah, "La banlieue côté filles," 103–5.

24. In 1790 the National Assembly voted to have the Catholic clergy take an oath of allegiance to the first French constitution and to confiscate church property for the state. Napoleon restored the tie between church and state in 1801 through a concordat with the pope that recognized Catholicism as the religion of most of France and reinstated priests as state employees; the pope agreed to renounce any claims to church property in France. Catholic schools revived their role during the nineteenth century, notably as practically the only source of education for young women. Private Catholic schools in France now receive government subsidies by a contract that stipulates their rights and obligations. A private Islamic school has just opened in Lille under a similar arrangement.

25. See the essay by Etienne Balibar, "Dissonances within *laïcité*," *Constellations* 11 (2004): 353–67.

26. Many opinions on this issue have appeared in the French press. See the selection from the newspaper *Libération* published in a collection titled *La laïcité dévoilée* (Paris: Editions de l'Aube, 2004).

27. See the work of Benjamin Stora, particularly *La gangrène et l'oubli: la mémoire de la guerre d'Algérie* (Paris: La Découverte, 1991) and *Le transfert d'une mémoire: de "l'Algérie française" au racisme anti-arabe* (Paris: La Découverte, 1999).

28. My reference here is to Le Pen and the Front national, but conservative members within the Stasi commission reportedly shared his views. See *New York Times*, 12 December 2003, 1 and 12.

29. Kramer, "Taking the Veil," 67; and *Le Monde*, 21 June 2005, 9 and 15.

30. See *Le Monde* of 3 and 4 September 2004. Unfortunately there was an intense flurry of media attention surrounding these young women.

31. Françoise Gaspard and Farhad Khosrokhavar, *Le foulard et la République* (Paris: La Découverte, 1995), 47.

32. Ibid., 59. The authors contend that for the majority of young Muslim women, a headscarf is an expression of individual liberty: "each girl does what she wants and it's her own business."

33. Françoise Gaspard and Farhad Khosrokhavar, "L'égalité des filles, avec ou sans voiles," in *Laïcité dévoilée*, 25; it first appeared in *Libération*, 8 December 1994. Françoise Gaspard was also the mayor of the suburban town of Dreux that came under attack by the Front national in local elections.

34. The parity law divided French feminists between those who supported a law based on sexual difference as an act of affirmative action, and those who opposed it and insisted that only reform of the whole representative system would permit respect for the principles of universal human rights.

35. Kramer, "Taking the Veil," 68.

36. See the treatment of male homosexuality and Islam by Malek Chebel in *L'esprit de sérail: mythes et pratiques sexuels au Maghreb* (Paris: Editions Payot et Rivages, 2003), 9–10, 19–68.

37. Written in language that treats the reader both as an adult and as a buddy, the seventy-page pocket-size guide contains a wealth of commonsense advice, practical information, and no-nonsense questions and answers. See the Web site niputesnisoumises.com.

38. "Towards a new feminist struggle," a tract for the 2005 International Women's Day demonstration, paraphrases the notion first elaborated by the utopian socialist philosopher Charles Fourier in the 1830s. The 8 March 2005 demonstrations, however, revealed divisions within French women's movements over the headscarf issue.

39. Charles Tilly refers to the "fable" in his introduction to Noiriel, *French Melting Pot*, vii; the other expression is Noiriel's (see note 16).

Breaking the Silence

PROLOGUE

I would never have imagined we could do it. To bring together on 8 March 2003 more than thirty thousand people in the streets of Paris, most of them from the suburbs, behind our slogan Ni Putes Ni Soumises—I would never even have dared to dream of such success.

For many years feminist associations had struggled to mobilize around their own traditional themes. And there we were, a handful of young women from the housing projects, with little political experience, who had managed to assemble some of the most diverse organizations in French society, political parties, unions, associations for women's rights, and various other groups! Public opinion suddenly discovered these women from the projects who were demonstrating to protest the daily violence they endured; everyone could glimpse the proud faces of women who were determined to break the taboos of a new form of sexism.

We were only eight marchers at the start, six young women and two young men, who set out—in a climate of indifference and distrust—on a five-week march to denounce gang rape and male violence. Our path through France included twenty-three stopovers, multiple press conferences, meetings with elected officials, and debates with people in the housing projects, all aiming to raise the awareness of this evil that was destroying our suburbs.

Two major events several months earlier had incited us to organize this march. One was the horrible crime that took place on 4 October 2002: the murder of Sohane, a young woman of eighteen, burned alive in the cellar of a housing project in Vitry-sur-Seine. Beautiful and rebellious, Sohane paid with her life for her refusal to conform to the gender norms of the suburbs, to the laws of brute force. Her older sister Kahina, despite her grief, her suffering, and outside pressure, refused to remain silent. With courage and determination (like another Kahina, famous in the history of the Berber people), she spoke out against the atrocity that had destroyed her family and vowed to make public the fate of young women in the projects.

Several months before that Samira Bellil had published *Dans l'enfer des tournantes*, a personal account of gang rapes, now a topic of public attention. We had often heard stories in our association meetings, stories of gang rape perpetrated by groups of young men against women who had refused to hide their femininity. But the pressure in the projects was so strong that the victims refused to speak out, and the neighborhood maintained its taboos. In revealing the facts, Samira's testimony—raw, direct and painful—acted like a bomb. She faced her struggle alone and told the whole story. I have great admiration for her and for her great humanity.[1] During meetings at each stopover of our march, she explained again and again that she could never pardon those who raped her, but she could understand how they came to act in this way, and the long, slow process of destruction that consumed these young men. By refusing to live with hatred, she taught us an extraordinary lesson. I am proud that she has become the symbolic center of our movement. Her book also helped open the eyes of women suffering the same horrors, giving them the strength to say "Enough!" The support and the direct experience of Kahina and Samira have strengthened our resolve to put an end to violence against women.

In my role as president of the National Federation of Solidarity Houses (Fédération nationale des maisons des potes) I managed, despite the skepticism and resistance of some of my co-workers, to convince a handful of militants of the need to organize a march to denounce publicly the actions of a minority of young men whose behavior was ruining our lives in the projects. We began by organizing the Estates General of Neighborhood Women, an unheard-of moment for these normally silent women to speak out. Then came the moment for our march, the March by Neighborhood Women for Equality and against the Ghetto. Just twenty years earlier, in 1983, the Beur

---

1. [Trans.] On 6 September 2004 Samira Bellil, thirty-three, died of cancer. Her women friends considered the book (2002) about the gang rapes she suffered at age thirteen to be an act of courage, but it divided the Muslim community and brought her under attack by Islamic fundamentalists.

March had taken place. It represented the first collective initiative by young people from immigrant families, both to protest the outburst of racist crimes against them, and to claim their identity as full citizens in the French Republic. The March by Neighborhood Women in February and March 2003 clearly marked the beginning of a collective consciousness. A slow process of social breakdown has taken place in the suburbs, the origins of which are to be found in the problems of unemployment that severely affect suburban youth; in the rampant poverty among families, no matter what their origins; in the cultural and political exclusion that has marginalized the inhabitants of the projects; in the daily acts of discrimination against young people from immigrant families; and finally, in the violence that is the lot of any abandoned community. The first victims of this slow drift toward the ghetto have been women. Gang rape is only the most visible sign of this process. The daily lives of women are also marred by a whole series of humiliations and limitations. For the past several months they have begun to join us and say "Stop"! To assert that they are "feminine, even feminists, who want to wear skirts without being treated as 'bitches,'" as the Marseillais hip-hop singer Louisa so aptly says.

It is not our intention, it is not my intention, to stigmatize young men in the housing projects in any way. Not all of them have become macho, petty dealers who have turned the projects into lawless zones as they are so often represented in the media. But undeniably violence has made its way into normal life there and shifted their behavior.

I try to present a lucid viewpoint on our lives in the projects. If the reality is bitter, I still believe there is room for hope.

The law of silence (*l'omertà*)[2] is shattered. More and more young women, mothers, even young men listen to us and react. Now we must continue our struggle to effect change. "Let's act and move on" has become the rallying cry for all of us who want things to change. At long last.

2. [Trans.] The Italian term *omertà* refers to a rule or code that prohibits speaking out or informing on criminal activities, as in the Mafia's code of honor.

PART ONE

Social Breakdown in the Projects

Daughter of the Housing Projects

My own personal history undoubtedly influenced my under-standing of these young women's position. I was born in Auvergne, a reputedly austere region in central France where people are reserved but also capable of a profound and discreet generosity if you know how to earn it. To identify myself more precisely, I was born in Clermont-Ferrand, a working-class city steeped in popular culture, where almost everything revolved around the Michelin Tire factory. When I was a child, work, housing, schools, the very lives of a great many men and women in Clermont-Ferrand took on the rhythms of the factory. During these years, manufacturers treated their employees with a certain paternalism under the watchful eyes of the mayor, Roger Quillot, who was, I might add, a specialist on the writings of Albert Camus.[1] I am very attached to the region of

1. [Trans.] The French novelist and philosopher Albert Camus (1913–60) was born in Algeria and moved to France several years before

my birth and if, in the present debate over identity politics, I were asked to define myself in terms of a certain category, in the end I would call myself a "woman of Auvergne"!

I come from a rather typical North African family of ten children, six boys and four girls. My father was tough with all his children, and authoritarian and strict in terms of their upbringing—respect meant a lot to him and he imposed it and taught us to value it. Nevertheless, he made a clear distinction between how a girl should behave and what was expected of a boy. The gender differences in personal freedom of action were patently obvious: my oldest brother had nearly all the rights; my sisters and I almost none. As for housework, we had to do everything; he was never asked to do anything, except perhaps to assume his responsibilities as the eldest son. In this way the relations between my oldest brother and the other siblings became completely warped. Caught in this role and bound by patriarchal tradition, my brother found himself progressively isolated and, as he grew up, started a slow drift toward prison. While this drama left an indelible mark on the family, strange as it might seem, it also made relations with my oldest brother somewhat easier.

World War II. During the German occupation, Camus worked for the Resistance clandestine newspaper *Combat* and is best known for his enigmatic novel *L'étranger* (1942; *The Stranger*) that takes place in Algeria. His work evolved toward a philosophy of moral consciousness that put him in opposition to communism and existentialism, defended notably by Jean-Paul Sartre. He was awarded the Nobel Prize for Literature in 1957.

AN ORDINARY CHILDHOOD
IN AN IMMIGRANT FAMILY

My sisters and I could not leave the house when we pleased, a situation many women of my generation faced whether or not they were from immigrant families. For example, when youth workers organized camps in the countryside, my brother had an easier time getting permission to go, while for us girls, such trips required endless discussion and negotiation. We had the same problem for the movies, where we had to begin discussions two weeks before going. And it was often my mother who interceded on our behalf, taking on the role of both advocate and peacekeeper as far as I was concerned. She was continually smoothing things out.

This distribution of roles was in fact classic and common in our milieu. But, like many of my girlfriends, I did not understand why this gender difference existed and I considered it an injustice. I constantly challenged it and during my adolescence I never stopped questioning it. Thus my father and I had harsh and frequent clashes. By contrast, my sisters were calmer and more given to discussion and negotiation and were able to maintain a dialogue with our parents.

My father had a rather simple idea of everyone's place in society: men and women were certainly equal before the law, but men belonged to the outside world and women to the private one at home! This was the conception of the world that he had inherited from his Berber education; it was a very common vision among immigrant workers. When my father arrived in France, how could he realize that this model was no longer accepted in the modern society in which he had come to live—a society where women could go out, work, and organize their lives—since he was settled in a housing project that sheltered only immigrant workers from North Africa like himself? Berber fathers like him came from a patriarchal and male chauvinist society where the men were obliged to provide for the needs of wives. In turn the women had to remain at home to raise the children. There was a division of labor within the couple: the man took charge of the family's financial needs through work and the wife stayed home to look after the children and manage the domestic space. Women never left home, except to do errands and pick up the children at school. Daughters were supposed to follow the same model. My father would never have allowed his wife to work outside the home. He would have experienced this as a personal inability to provide for his family, calling into question his place as head of the household. And then, there was the question of what others would see or say, of public opinion.

My mother suffered a great deal from this situation. She was twenty-two years younger than my father and longed for some financial independence, for some freedom of decision, and for some pocket money to buy herself a "few trinkets," as she said. This subject often provoked small disputes at home. Among ourselves we sisters and brothers were able to settle this problem later on, by sending her some money every month.

Yet I don't at all hold this against my father: he sincerely believed he was doing the right thing for his daughters. Even though I was very much afraid of him, I tried instead to understand why he reacted this way. I always had a special curiosity about him, a desire to know more about his family history, and about life in Algeria, his country of origin.[2] As my parents never had enough money to take all their children during summer visits, only a few of my sisters and brothers went there, and it is a country I know very poorly and discovered later in my life. My father's emigration experience is rather ordinary. He left Aït Yussef in the mountains of Little Kabylia and arrived in France in 1955 to look for work in construction. My mother joined him in 1960 after their marriage. She was sixteen, and she had her first child very rapidly. Then other children followed, when she was seventeen, eighteen, nineteen years old. When my parents arrived—like many other immigrants who responded to France's need for more workers—they were "parked" in a transit city. Herbet, the housing project where my parents settled and where I grew up, was located in the southeastern suburbs of Clermont-Ferrand. It was not a large complex but rather a small popular neighborhood, a half-hour from the city center, and it housed one hundred and fifty families. It was, in fact, a shantytown that had been transformed into temporary housing in the late 1960s and underwent repeated refurbishing. I remember it as a prototypical village where everyone knew and helped everybody else, and the children grew up together. Even though the foreign population had been grouped together, I never felt we lived in a ghetto. Even so, 90 percent of our housing project was populated by Algerian immigrants, all of whom held residence

2. [Trans.] As noted in the introduction, France conquered the city of Algiers in 1830 and colonized the vast territory of Algeria during the nineteenth century. Algeria was considered an integral part of France until 1962.

permits. Just opposite, two streets away, was a neighborhood called la Condamine where a large Portuguese community lived.

From childhood I realized certain things weren't right. For example, there was a slaughterhouse near the place we were living and it swarmed with rats. At school, along with the other children from the housing project, we were called the "kids from Herbet," which was a way of identifying our neighborhood as the Arab quarter. I did not understand these distinctions and these labels because I never felt any problem of identity. To be sure, I was named Fadela, but I was born in France, in Clermont-Ferrand in 1964. Like many other kids, I was lulled to sleep with fairy tales, stories, and legends in which monsters played a large part. Like many other schoolchildren, I read *Poil de carotte* (*Carrot Top*) and *Le petit prince* (*The Little Prince*) and I adored listening to the story on tape of Peter and the wolf, read in the marvelous voice of Gérard Philippe (I was in love with him for a long time). Christmas was also an important holiday for us—and for all the other families in the projects—and each year I waited impatiently for Santa Claus to bring gifts and sweets. Like everyone else, my brothers and sisters and I made bets with candy as to who would be the first to see him. We spent some very short nights! But the magic always worked when we awoke in the morning and discovered the gifts spread out in secret. It was the same at Easter time. My mother scattered Easter eggs and chocolate chickens and bells around our little back-yard. It was like a treasure hunt, and I must admit that of all of us, it was my mother who had the greatest fun watching us search everywhere and cry out with joy when we found a treasure.

So on occasion I was surprised to find that others perceived me as different, as coming from somewhere else. Over time such thoughts took form and became discrimination, exclusion, racism—the Far Right's favorite themes. But, deep down, I knew with certainty that this was not France. My own France—a view shared by a great number of people from immigrant families—is the France of the Enlightenment, the France of the republic, the France of Marianne, of the supporters of Alfred Dreyfus, of the Paris Commune, of the Resistance.[3] In short, the France of liberty, equality, and fraternity, a secular France where the only principle that prevails is the advancement of social conscience and nothing else. But by chance it was in France's republican melting pot—the school I attended as a child—that I truly felt for the first time that I was a foreigner. It occurred one day when a teacher, who wanted to make a list of foreign students in the class and who certainly believed she was doing the right thing, asked me to raise my hand. And yet, according to the law issued from the Evian accords, I was a French citizen.[4]

My parents themselves remained Algerian—my father chose to do so at the time of Algerian independence; one of my brothers, born before 1962, still holds a residence permit; and my oldest sister obtained French nationality through marriage. My family is thus a real puzzle of nationalities, much like many other immigrant families.

We lived in Herbet in relative poverty. But my mother was infinitely resourceful. To make our life easier she did her utmost

3. [Trans.] Amara refers to republican triumphs over threats to the country's values, including the Dreyfus affair, a crisis of religious intolerance and discrimination in late nineteenth-century France.

4. [Trans.] The Evian accords, signed in 1962, marked France's recognition of Algerian independence; they included safeguards for Algerians in France and for French settlers and their property in Algeria.

to manage with what she had. She invented games, baked sweet cakes, sang popular songs for us by Enrico Macias, Claude François, Sheila, Rabah Dreiassa, and each with the appropriate accent, no less! At home, as was true in the rest of the housing project, we lacked many things and we could not eat meat at every meal. Even so, there were always potatoes on our plates, cooked in many different ways. And I confess that I never grew tired of them!

I remember my father coming home on Friday evenings and counting his wages—there were no paychecks then—he would make small piles: one for the food budget, another for miscellaneous expenses, a third for savings, in case of emergencies. These are memories that mark your life. I hold this image of my father: serious, painstaking, someone who never smiled. My mother was just the opposite: almost childlike, always smiling, and sociable. Her gaiety compensated for my father's somber temperament.

SHORTENED SCHOOLING
AND CAREER OPTIONS

Trapped at home, I tried to make my way to freedom in the outside world. But I never found the means to succeed in what school offered. Instead, I had a chaotic school career, as many other young people in my neighborhood did. School always seemed so disconnected from our life outside. I read a great deal—my mother would say, "My daughter always has her head in books"—but I was bored sitting in a classroom. I had gotten it into my head that I would prepare a baccalaureate in literature because French was the only subject that interested me; in other subjects, I was hopeless and undisciplined. In fact, I was physically present in class but constantly thinking about something else! Immersed in those childhood dreams that carried me away into a brilliant future, I imagined becoming a star dancer in the Ballets du XXe siècle directed by the great Maurice Béjart. How many classes flicked through my head while I dreamed of a *pas de deux* with the wonderful dancer Jorge Donn! But things turned out differently. In any case, I did not understand, for example, why we could not talk in school about real problems, about life. I remember the death of a kid in the projects where the police had been involved. I had tried to talk with my teacher about why the cops were allowed to get away with such brutality. We all knew young men who had gone to prison for theft, and the image we had of justice was of a double standard. Only much later, in the context of a project involving Solidarity House and the Youth Recreation Center run by Bob Sametier and his team of policemen, was I able to revise my image of the French police. I realized that most of the police were dedicated women and men who took risks so that everyone could benefit from a fundamental right in a democracy, the right to security. The only answer the teacher gave me was "We don't talk about this type of subject in class. We are here to learn and to work." I began to tune out of school.

I was expelled from secondary school at age sixteen and directed toward "the real world." To keep me from total alienation (*la galère*),[5] my mother pushed me to get a vocational

5. [Trans.] This new term from the inner city or suburbs, as Richard L. Derderian explains, "is a highly volatile sense of detachment and frustration among suburban youth produced by an environment that excludes, alienates, and stigmatizes" them. *North Africans in Contemporary France: Becoming Visible* (New York: Palgrave Macmillan, 2004), 148. See also the film *La Haine* (1996), set in the suburbs north of Paris, which depicts the violence this alienation may trigger.

diploma *(certificat d'aptitude professionnelle)* as an office worker. Since my father's financial situation had somewhat improved, he was able to enroll me in a private Catholic girls' school. Knowing my rebellious temperament, he did not want me hanging around outside the house. He was afraid I'd come up against the court of neighborhood opinion, people would say I talked too much, and I was always protesting. He knew such a reputation had consequences: men would never ask to marry you. So for him, the only successful path for a woman was to marry and to have a family. I did not fit this model at all, so I needed a makeover.

The Catholic girls' school was a shock for me. The rules were very strict and every morning we had to say prayers. It was a requirement that was not negotiable. So I bent myself to the rules, but as a Muslim I recited my prayers in Arabic. My teachers did not appreciate this, and their reflections soon turned into judgments. Intolerance takes many forms. I had to repeat the year, failed my vocational exam, and ended up in the national unemployment agency. On a daily basis, as a way of hanging on, I read. This immoderate taste for reading was a legacy from my teacher Madame Peyron, who had given me my first book. Since then I have never stopped reading. From Victor Hugo to Alfred de Musset, from Alexander Dumas to Emile Zola, from Martin Luther King to Gandhi, by way of Marguerite Yourcenar, Hermann Hesse, Khalil Gibran, and many others. I especially liked the talented Kateb Yacine, who evoked for me the story of my parents.[6]

6. [Trans.] The Algerian novelist and poet Kateb Yacine (1929–89) wrote his early work in French, rather than his native Arabic. *Kateb* means writer in Arabic.

During this period you signed in every month at the employment office. Watching everyone line up to justify the meager unemployment benefits they received made me sick, especially for older people who looked so exhausted as they waited. I found it scandalous that a country like France could not find work for them. I was ready to let go the thousand francs they handed out at the time in order to escape such humiliation. I knew my life was not going to be easy, particularly as I was starting with few qualifications. But since I had brought this on myself, I had to take responsibility for it. I struggled on by stringing together several fixed-term contracts and various types of part-time work.

SHOCKED INTO BECOMING A MILITANT

I really found myself through collective action. My commitment as a militant began with the shock caused by the death of one of my brothers when I was fourteen years old. It happened in 1978, when my little brother Malik, the youngest in the family, was run over by a drunken driver. I saw how the cops were able to mistreat people simply because they were Arabs. When my mother saw her son on the ground, she fell apart and began to shriek with pain. The cops arrived and one of them caught her and shook her. I was standing next to my brother, holding him in my arms and talking to him to tell him Mother was there and not to worry. When I looked up, I saw this cop roughing up my mother and bullying my father. Then, after the ambulance had taken my little brother to the hospital, I went over to hit the cop and shout insults at him. I screamed and forbade him to speak to my parents this way. I can still hear his response: "These *bougnoule*s

(Arabs) piss me off!"[7] It was like electroshock: I completely blew up. Young people from the nearby project were out of their minds with fury and began attacking the drunken driver and roughing him up. The police protected him and, instead of trying to calm things, began to call us "dirty Arabs" and shout that no Arabs were going to order them about.

My little brother died later that night at the hospital. He was five years old. This episode left its mark on the housing project. For a long time after this event there was tension between the police and the young people of our neighborhood. When the cops descended on the project, they came not to teach us a lesson but to clamp down on us in a violent way. They would break into people's homes by knocking down the doors, pick up some young man, and haul him off to prison. During this period vans of the special riot police would suddenly block off the two entrances to the housing project; they would take out their billy clubs and cut loose. During my entire adolescence I lived with this image of cops swooping down on the project to make some family unhappy. But there was such strong solidarity that when they questioned one of us, it affected the whole housing project. So even if a few kids were doing stupid things, it was hard on all of us.

And so for a long time Herbet, our housing project, had a reputation that clouded the life of its inhabitants. Many young people of my generation were victims of discrimination. During this period, social mobility through schooling was extremely difficult. Very few continued on to the university since it was too expensive. Because I could not agree to this injustice, this outsider's view that systematically reduced me to my social and

---

7. [Trans.] In French slang, *bougnoules* is a very offensive term for Arabs.

ethnic origins, I had to do everything in my power to change it. I wanted to prove that despite our differences we had the ability to live together, and that this was possible in a secular republic with full citizenship rights.

Thus, after the death of my little brother, I decided to make something happen. At this time one of the rare environments where young women had a sense of being on an equal footing with men was in the housing project. So this is where I took my stand. At seventeen I organized with some women friends a "civic march" to register young people to vote. The objective was twofold: to demonstrate our sentiment of belonging to the nation by participating in the elections, but also to gain the respect of local elected officials. Four hundred young people joined us, and our delegation was received by the mayor. This was itself a first victory. Soon afterward, in 1982, we created an association with the help of the municipality, the Association des femmes pour l'échange intercommunautaire (women's association for ethnic relations). Our motivation was to create a space for collective exchange and solidarity, to enhance daily life in the projects. Our goal was to have our fathers, mothers, and all young people help promote our neighborhood in order to change its public image, and to give everyone a stake in our collective work.

Then there was the Beur March. During the winter of 1983, a small group of young men from the Minguettes, a suburban neighborhood of Lyon, decided to organize a march to denounce the racism that immigrants' children experienced. At that time, not a month went by without some racist crime being committed, either by fascists or by the cops. The organizers of the march had the support of Father Christian Delorme, a priest working in the housing projects who had a major role in the initiative's success. The march had an enormous impact both in the projects and on the rest of French society. For the first time, immigrants' sons began to denounce the hatred that targeted them and demanded their integration into French society. Like my friends, I participated when the march stopped over in Clermont-Ferrand. But I did not go to the national demonstration when they reached Paris because my father was totally opposed to my going. I had to watch it on television.

But afterward, when groups assembled for the next march, I didn't join in because I couldn't identify with them. I felt that the men were too "macho": they wanted the women to march but hadn't the slightest interest in equality between men and women. When we told them that they should change their behavior, that the march should include both Beurs and Beurettes, they turned a deaf ear. They could not accept the idea that women might demand something. I preferred investing my energy in my own neighborhood, where my women friends and I put together a plan to fix up housing that had fallen in disrepair. The electricity was so substandard and the buildings were so damaged that a catastrophe might happen at any moment. We fought to have the town set aside a budget for substantial restoration. We also worked a lot on job placement, because unemployment had already had such disastrous effects on these neighborhoods.

JOINING SOS RACISME

It was during this period that I met several activists from SOS Racisme. This association, well known because of its phrase "Touche pas à mon pote" (Hands off my buddy), was created in December 1984 in the wake of the second Beur march. This march, called Convergence 84, sought to promote solidarity among all French people, but the march itself was only partially successful: the Beur movement was by then divided between those young people who favored integration and working with political parties on the Left, and those who wanted to build an autonomous North African movement. However, the little yellow hand symbol and slogan of SOS Racisme rapidly gained widespread support among young people in France. My father and I watched the news every day on television. In fact, the news report was the only program we could watch together. It was not worth even trying to watch films, because whenever there were scenes with actors kissing, zap! we changed the channel. So I first saw SOS Racisme on the little screen: in contrast to the Beur movement, it displayed real ethnic diversity. I was delighted to see whites, blacks, and Rebeus together, all demanding the right to live in a society of equality and fraternity.[8]

I had to wait until I could take part. For a long time my father opposed the idea because he thought a young woman had no place in these movements. There was always a terrible family fight when women wanted to become activists, so they ended up joining secretly. I became a member of SOS Racisme at the end of 1986 thanks to the help of two girlfriends, Khadija and Maryse (who has since died). They had an extraordinary role in my life— reflecting one of those chance encounters that help you rise above difficulties. As they both came regularly to my home, my parents were fond of them and trusted them when they took me out.

8. [Trans.] As she describes the group's composition—*Blanc, Black, Beur*—Amara substitutes Rebeus for Beur, an ethnic label North African youth now disclaim. For a discussion of these terms of suburban slang, see the introduction.

Thanks to these friends I participated in evening meetings, and with their help I also traveled to Paris to attend the meetings of the national council of SOS Racisme. It is important to understand what it meant for my father, a Berber, to see his daughter leave for Paris and spend the night away from home. He was afraid of what people would say and of what stupid things I might do. He tended to become stricter when my sisters and I asked him for permission to go out, since he had to control everything. Without Maryse and Khadija, therefore, I would never have been able to go to Paris and become an activist. Thanks to them and to other militants such as Mohammed Abdi or Malek Boutih, I learned how to emancipate myself. At SOS Racisme everyone was convinced that women should have the same commitment to freedom as men. It was so rare to meet a Beur who spoke of freedom for women. Little by little through my activism I learned to question the rigid education I had received. Even though I had protested against it earlier, the gender roles it taught were part of me. Just as an example, there was the fact that I cleaned the house without finding it abnormal that my younger brothers never did so.

My commitment to SOS Racisme also initiated me into a political culture about which I knew very little. Coming from the projects, you lack the tools you need to decode events and analyze their social context. During the Algerian War of Independence my father had taken sides with the FLN,[9] but he had little understanding of how French political life worked. I

9. [Trans.] The FLN is the Front de libération nationale, one of two rival movements working for Algerian independence. As an Algerian immigrant worker in France, Amara's father had been called upon to aid the cause. See the introduction.

had had courses in civics at school, but they had bored me because our teacher was tough and stern. In the following years, I recognized that, thanks to him, I had learned the basics about how the republic operated.

In 1988 we worked on founding a solidarity house (maison des potes). The National Federation of Solidarity Houses had been launched that year by militants from SOS Racisme with the aim of transforming the suburbs' negative image and highlighting the positive effects of local initiatives. Today, this federation encompasses nearly three hundred neighborhood associations. For years I had been looking for exactly this, and I threw myself into the movement. Transforming local neighborhoods was the only thing that interested me. Later I became a permanent staff member of this association.

My commitment was no doubt fairly unusual for a young woman of my age. But to varying degrees our entire generation was getting involved in public life. This fact helped young women move toward more personal freedom and gave young men another view of them.

When I was an adolescent, boys and girls in a neighborhood grew up together. At school and outside the family circle, and on excursions too, girls and boys weren't kept apart as they are today. The word "respect" still applied not only to parents and our elders, but also to relations between boys and girls. No boy in the neighborhood would dare insult a girl or lay a hand on her. If he saw her outside the project with an unknown group of boys, for example, he might tell her brother but would never think of showing his disapproval publicly or settling the problem by himself. Girls and boys would even collude, often closing their eyes and saying nothing.

The duty to remain a virgin obviously weighed heavily on young women's sexuality. But at the same time the struggle by the Beur movement, strengthened by SOS Racisme, also allowed a measure of freedom to the young women who participated. Hundreds of women suddenly had a new freedom of movement and the possibility of choosing their partners. While little was said officially in their families, a tacit agreement existed: as long as the young woman did not exhibit herself publicly, she could have a love life. In this way foreign-born women often married men from different backgrounds. I think mixed marriages were more common then than they are today. Even then they were easier for men who, according to our patriarchal system, inherit the family name and transmit it to the next generation.

2

The Status of Women
in the 1990s

The first hints of change came around 1990. We sensed that relations between young women and men were strained after we set
up a women's center during the early months of Solidarity
House's presence in Clermont-Ferrand. Girls began to come in,
complaining that they were unhappy because they wanted to go
out in the evenings, but their fathers opposed this on the grounds
that people would talk. You had to stay clear of the court of neighborhood opinion. These young women came for advice about
their freedom of movement, about going to the movies from
time to time. We had all encountered these same problems, but
we had been able to resolve them by ourselves. We had fought to
gain a little freedom, but these women no longer had the strength
to fight. In our families, dialogue and communication had been
possible because children still talked with their parents. In these
girls' families, lies and silence had come to govern the relations
between parents and children.

GROWING MALE OPPRESSION

At first we didn't notice much difference in gender relations. As the months passed, young women's complaints to the women's center began to change. They came by more and more often to talk about the economic constraints that weighed on them within the family. Most of the young women who were fortunate enough to have jobs saw their wages confiscated. Their contribution to the family income was no longer negotiable, as it had been, but had become an obligation to turn over almost all of their salary. The loss of personal wages was a threat to their independence. Buying makeup or beauty creams, going to the hairdresser, going shopping, all these innocent-seeming things became difficult. Such details, while they remain details, were with hindsight evidence of this slow breakdown.

Then came the period of physical violence. We had to handle a growing number of cases of girls who had run away from their homes and needed emergency shelter. Within the space of two to three years, the situation totally fell apart. During this time older brothers had come on the scene. The nature of the pressure young women of immigrant origin felt had by then changed: the constraints were no long those imposed by tradition or by the family, but those exercised by young men.

This deterioration took place during a period of mass unemployment that hit the housing projects hard. Immigrant workers were the first ones to be laid off in industries that were being restructured, and fathers found themselves deprived of work and social status. Their forced idleness completely upset their roles within the family and undermined their authority as fathers. Up until then they had had a monopoly on authority, since they were the ones who established the rules of family life and arbitrated disputes between brothers and sisters. Today, fathers are absent, a fact that emerges clearly from debates on suburban discontent, in which the main questions concern mothers, older brothers, but rarely fathers. Now the eldest son has taken over; he rules the family. He has physically replaced the father in his protective and repressive roles. Mothers continue to look after the education of younger children, to transmit family values, but now the eldest son decides conflicts within the family. He has assumed responsibility for teaching family values to younger sisters and for policing their conduct outside the home to ensure that they behave.

So, once young men had claimed this authority within the family, they began to exercise it within the housing projects. Their mission was clear: to protect their sisters from predators and to preserve their virginity until marriage. This authority did not yet extend to other young women in the project, just to sisters. Families then organized around the son, absorbing his self-assigned task, the protection of his sisters. Everyone closed their eyes, pretending that this was in the young women's best interests. And these women saw the freedom they had acquired during the Beur movements and antiracist demonstrations of the 1980s become more and more restricted.

Little by little the pressure on young women's daily lives in the projects turned to oppression. Their comings and goings were controlled, and their freedom to leave home was reduced to nothing. During the rare times when they were allowed to go out, they had a curfew. No more chances to go out alone. They now had to be accompanied by girlfriends who were acceptable to the family, and sometimes even by a brother, ostensibly there to protect them. At the same time, strict control was imposed on the male company these young women kept. Inside the housing project barriers were erected. Outside the family, mixed-sex company—*mixité*—was forbidden. From year to year, girls were more and more confined at home as their destiny. Those who tried to continue their studies had a real battle on their hands: why bother, since a young woman's natural and inevitable goal in life had once again become marriage?

The next step was to extend this male power from the oldest brother to all the young men in the projects. Their surveillance was systematically directed against the "tribe of young women." Now the honor of each family and of the project was in the hands of these young men. Since the honor consisted in preserving women's virginity, these young men became the collective guardians of this treasure. People no longer said "This is so-and-so's daughter" but rather "This girl is from such-and-such neighborhood," based on the assumption that these boys had the right to control her life and the company she kept.

THE NEW MALE GUARDIANS
OF THE HOUSING PROJECTS

The change in boys' behavior toward girls was slow but absolute. The more time passed, the more the government neglected the housing projects, the more young men became radicalized. This was especially the case among unemployed men who hung out on the grounds below the high-rise housing, those who "held up the walls," as we say. These guys were always together, stewing on their resentments and failures; they became authoritarian and then turned to verbal violence and insults against girls.

Whenever they found young women outside the projects, they would order them to go home by threatening to tell their brothers what these girls had done, where they had been seen, and in whose company. Thus the men in the family, who were supposedly protecting the girls, kept track of them.

The next step was direct intervention. Confident that they were exercising their authority by bothering a young woman, especially if she was in the company of a young man from another neighborhood, young men would not hesitate to assert their "right of possession" by affirming "This girl is from my project. You've got nothing to do with her." Girls had no right to defend themselves; they were expected to go home and wait for the report that would unfailingly be given to their brother.

Already by the mid-1990s I was growing more and more worried by the violence that had begun to spread in the suburbs, linked to their social breakdown. But the most frightening aspect of this process had been to observe that more and more boys were taking possession of girls' bodies. As a result, these young women were imprisoned at home. From then on, they were forbidden to dress or to use makeup as they wished. Boys imposed their own law on how girls could dress. No more tight-fitting jeans and T-shirts, because they were too provocative and revealing of women's femininity. The young men were unrelenting: women who dared to break the rules were treated as "whores." During my adolescence, it was considered natural for us to wear short skirts, tight-fitting jeans, low-cut blouses, and short T-shirts. No man would have dared to make offensive remarks. This showing off of our femininity was observed from afar, but accepted, even provoked at times in a kind of seduction played out between girls and boys.

Today, and for the past ten years, these young men experience femininity as a provocation and as something reprehensible. As a way of getting their own back, girls who do better at school manage to go out in the evenings, thanks to their studies. It's also true that they would rather go out with a student or someone who works, and they refuse guys who hang around the projects. The latter know it and take offense. So they seem determined to make the girls feel guilty and pay for the desire they provoke. Hence these boys asserted their right to make rules of behavior for the girls in their project, and to enforce them against those who do not obey, especially those who are comfortable in their own femininity. They took control of their neighborhood, as if the fact of living there allowed them to possess everything inside, including the young women.

Even though only a minority of boys exhibit such extremely violent behavior, a large majority of guys in the projects have adopted this hypervirility. Respect for others and solidarity no longer mean anything; only the law of the strongest and the affirmation of their manhood remain. To exist, "they put their balls on the line." The only way for them to be recognized both outside and inside the projects is to act macho and violent. Of course this behavior affects their relations with young women. In their representation of the world, a man must affirm himself by banging his fist on the table, by being very tough with his wife or his girlfriend. As a result they have to display this macho attitude toward all women. And those who do not follow the rules—those who do not want to do so or who are more fragile, called *bouffons* (clowns)—incur the same violence young women do. For homosexuals, life is terrible. No one in the projects talks about homosexuality. When someone is discovered to be gay, his life becomes hell.

WHY DID THINGS CHANGE?

How did we reach this point, since the two previous decades showed relations between young women and men moving toward greater equality, as they are among young people in the rest of French society? Several contributing factors are specific to life in the projects.

First of all, as social injustice increased during this period, young men were its first victims. The fact that their social origins were modest, most often foreign, and that they lived in a problem neighborhood, meant that every day they met up with strong discrimination that had its roots in prejudice against ethnic minorities and in racism. When they looked for work, housing, or more simply a club to go to outside the neighborhood, even just a walk around the center of town, they had a negative label immediately stuck to their skin. And it made its way deep inside, especially if they were children of immigrants. Perhaps they thought it was hereditary, because we of the previous generation had already felt it, as our parents had before us. Each generation has reacted in its own way: our parents remained silent, almost invisible. They worked, they went home, and they lived for the idea of returning to their country of origin. My generation, while we were going to school, we began to think and to act. Today, almost all the boys have retreated into the only space over which they have some control, the housing projects.

Another factor that allows us to understand this change is the fact that in immigrant families patriarchy is embedded in the way the family operates, with the result that all male members have always benefited from greater freedom of movement than have females. They can do whatever they want, and at home there are few constraints imposed on them. By observing my mother I understood all of this. She would bend over backward for her six sons. She loved her daughters, of course, but her sons were something else! My father shared this attitude. My parents always made their daughters assume responsibilities from which their sons were exempt. I do not hold it against them; they were conditioned to act in this way by their culture. But I was astonished to find this same way of functioning in families of French stock. Thus in the housing projects, even where women work outside the home and seem more free and independent, the law of the strongest is imposed in all family homes. Isn't this strange? In these families boys have been so spoiled, so overprotected, that they are incapable of fighting for themselves outside the home. Once they escape from parental control, some adopt the norms of the projects, while others—by choice or not—slide into delinquency.

Theirs is a schizophrenic life: they are kings within their family and nobodies outside the home. The absence of outside recognition fosters their sense of being excluded and rejected. If they are the sons of immigrants, a feeling of great injustice fuels their sense of not belonging to the nation. And if they belong to the third generation, they register it even more keenly. Such absence of outside recognition has generated incredible rage. In reaction, unable to come to grips with their exclusion, these young men exercise their mastery in the only space they know. Rather than turn against French society and the symbols of the republic, they oppress their sisters and all girls within the limited space of the projects.

3

Between Invisibility and Rebellion

Young women reacted rapidly to the increase in hypermasculinity and male violence. Isolated, each woman reacted differently or adapted her behavior to the new situation.

THE SUBMISSIVE, THE MANNISH, AND THE INVISIBLE

One type of behavior applies to young women who have internalized the return to reactionary patriarchal traditions and accepted masculine control over their lives. At home and in the projects, they conform to patriarchal society's "ideal" image of the submissive woman, the new social and gender norm. This model programs young women to become homemakers and came under attack from feminist movements during the 1970s. They stay at home, look after their younger brothers and sisters, help their mothers, and do the housework—they play at being dutiful daughters. They are taught how to run a household and trained to become good wives and mothers. In my opinion, this is total regression. They do not engage in a process of emancipation through education that would allow them afterward to work, to become financially independent, to affirm themselves, in fact to have the "right to choose," as we say. And then, outside, when exposed to an open society, some of these young women completely change their behavior. When they leave the projects, it's all waiting there, everything forbidden to them: men, movies, fashion, freedom. So they overconsume: they dress up like cool chicks, use heavy makeup, and try to pick up boys. For some of these girls the disconnect is too abrupt and they slip into prostitution or drugs. But generally speaking, to live in two such different worlds—at home in the projects, where young women must conform to the roles men want them to play, lowering their eyes when men look at them, and in the outside world, which seems to them a world of freedom—is extremely difficult for an adolescent girl to manage.

A second type of behavior involves young women who want to resemble men and force others to respect them. They adopt mannish attitudes, tactics, and gear. There are all-girl gangs in the projects, using violence as a means of expression, dressing in jogging clothes and sneakers, all-purpose unisex clothes that hide their femininity. These young women are violent in their language and behavior: they use extortion, they pick fights—even with young men—and they are quick to use insults or their fists. No tender gestures that might be perceived as a sign of weakness. They are sometimes worse than the young men, because they can be tougher and more sadistic than males. They think and live like the worst machos, they act as if they were "putting their balls on the line." In order to exist and to earn respect, they believe they've got to hit harder than the guys around them.

The third type of behavior is invisibility. It links young women who decided that their life was not in the projects and became ghosts there. They walk through a project as if it holds no meaning in their lives, on their way between home and school or university, and no one sees them come and go. These invisible young women do not live in the projects' public spaces or participate in local associations. They have only one thing in mind: complete their education and get out of the projects. Some live in constant fear of not being able to finish schooling, if their parents or their brother suddenly forbid them to do so. In our neighborhood today, to leave the family home overnight and sleep elsewhere, even to go to university classes, is unthinkable. When I was an adolescent, even if our parents did not take kindly to the idea of seeing their daughters study in Paris or in the provinces, they still did not prevent them from leaving and were very proud when they would return with their diploma. At that time it was less difficult to persuade them of the importance of continuing education. Today, more and more young women are pulled out of school: to help at home, perhaps, or to be sent back to the home country on the grounds of real or supposed bad behavior, or to be subjected to forced marriage, imposed by a family fearful of dishonor. The pressure on these girls is so strong that they often end by accepting. How many of them first thought that marriage was a passport to great freedom before finding themselves trapped.[1]

1. "The French government commission on integration revealed that there have been about 7,000 forced marriages in France in the past three years." Sylvia Poggioli on *NPR* News, 6 December 2004. Many of the young women are French citizens sent by their parents to

Forced marriages still occur in some African, Turkish, or North African communities, and we gathered testimony from many young women faced with this situation. As we were preparing for the estates general of women from the suburbs, a young woman told us about one of her friends:

"We had known each other for a very long time; we grew up together. She went out a lot and had some freedom. But her parents saw her as the girl who turns out badly. And then there's the pressure from those around them, who start to talk. So one day, the father went to see the mother and said this daughter had shamed the family. The mother cried, of course, and then all the pressure began; her mother, her brothers, everyone was on her back. From one day to the next, the situation changed. She no longer had the right to do anything. This situation lasted for months, months of conflict about everything and nothing. The moment finally came when she cracked and agreed to meet the suitors. One, then two, then three, and more until her mother said 'Stop.' Bitterly disappointed, she ended up accepting the fifth because he was younger, a little more open than the others. They dated a little, not too long, and then after a month, the parents organized a traditional marriage. From this day the reproaches and the quarrels began. They had a child and then the situation got worse. She was beaten. Her parents, of course, knew about this and felt guilty. For this reason they finally accepted a divorce. But by that time there was no family dishonor, since the guy was at fault and my friend had married

----

North Africa to marry older men, who gain French (and European Union) citizenship as part of the bargain.

according to tradition. I believe this story says a lot about family hypocrisy."[2]

THOSE WHO WEAR THE HEADSCARF

Among the young women in the projects there are those who seek recognition in a kind of return to ethnic community life, and in particular by turning to Islam for their identity. Some of them wear the headscarf by choice in the spirit of religious practice. But others have been subjected to pressures emanating from parents, religious leaders, or the projects. As someone who is very attached to fundamental freedoms, I think religious practice is legitimate when it is a personal choice, without pressure or constraint, but above all when it respects the norms of a secular society.

It is possible, in fact, to distinguish different categories of young women who wear the headscarf. First of all, there are those who wear it because they believe that the fact that they practice their religion affords them a legitimate existence. They are Muslim, they identify themselves as such, and they have the impression of being recognized and respected. They wear the headscarf as a banner.

But there are many young women who, forbidden any outward display of femininity, wear the headscarf above all as armor, supposed to protect them from male aggression. Indeed, women who wear the headscarf are never bothered by young men, who

2. Testimony collected in the *Livre blanc des femmes des quartiers* (working paper by neighborhood women), available at Solidarity House [in Paris].

lower their eyes in front of them; covered by the headscarf, these girls are in their view untouchable. Most of the girls who wear a headscarf to protect themselves take it off when they leave the projects. They always carry a bag into which they can slip it, together with a makeup kit—they are called *filles-cabas* (shopping-bag girls). Under their "armor" they wear tight-fitting clothes, low-necked blouses, but these clothes are not to be seen in the projects. This is such a terrible thing to imagine in a free country.

Finally, the third category of women who wear the headscarf includes those whom I call "soldiers of green fascism." In general these are women who attended university and who, behind this emblematic headscarf, fight for a social project that is dangerous for our democracy. These are not disturbed kids, troubled or searching for an identity, who wear the headscarf because it shows they belong to a community. No, these are real militants! They often begin their justification of wearing the headscarf by explaining that, in their view, it is part of a process of emancipation. It bothers me to hear them talk about freedom of expression because behind this symbol is a project for a different society than our own: a fascist-like society that has nothing to do with democracy.

In our countries of origin, now as in the past, the headscarf is not a sign of women's liberation. Women have been attacked with acid for refusing to wear it. Algerian feminists and many other women in Muslim countries, who fought to take it off in the name of freedom, have paid a heavy price. Women of my generation—including those who are practicing Muslims like myself—have fought against the headscarf because it has always been a symbol of women's oppression and confinement. And on our own ground today we are still battling these "soldiers of green fascism," who are a small minority but an extremely dangerous one.

THOSE WHO OFFER DAILY RESISTANCE

I could not round off this typology of young women's behavior without talking about those who resist and in fact represent the majority. They feel restive in the projects' oppressive atmosphere and resist by affirming their femininity. For young women of my generation, the fight for equality was the way we asserted ourselves, but these girls do not fight. They try to resist by being themselves, by continuing to wear revealing clothing, by dressing in fashion, by using makeup, sometimes outrageously. They want to live in a modern society, to exist as individuals, and to command personal respect on equal footing with young men.

In the housing projects there are many young women for whom makeup has become war paint, a sign of resistance. It is their way of fighting. It has nothing to do with the feminists of the 1970s who threw away their bras and led the war of the sexes! When I express surprise, they sometimes make an aggressive claim to their femininity. "They don't want me to wear makeup? Too bad, I paint my lips with lip pencil. God gave me a body that I inhabit and value. If this bothers them, then they can turn their eyes away."

These young women who resist are still in the majority in our neighborhood, but they pay the price every day. Guys willfully target them with their violence. They undergo daily harassment with insults and roughing up, and sometimes they are the first victims of rape. These young women's lives are often hell.

4

Sexuality in the Projects

Sexuality has always been a taboo subject in the housing projects. And precisely for this reason it has become a major issue: sex now figures in all conversations, all fantasies, but not comfortably, never openly.

Even when I was an adolescent, we never spoke about it with adults and we did not even talk about the problems of puberty, such as the onset of menstruation. A young woman would discover by herself her body and sexual development. Fortunately, we had a class in sexual education in secondary school during which we could ask questions that also provoked uncontrollable laughter. Life became more difficult for young women once menstruation began. The only comment that mothers made could be summed up with "That's the end of your seeing boys"! A young woman who menstruated could no longer hang around outside because she ran the risk of getting pregnant. This was the only statement related to their sexuality that young women heard. It was impossible to talk about all the rest, everything that concerned sexual behavior or love life.

FORBIDDEN SEXUALITY AS A SOURCE OF VIOLENCE

The situation I described has worsened over the past twenty years. Sexual education in the housing projects now involves little more than a furtive traffic in pornographic videos. Here once again, I believe, the national education system is of primary importance. To offset the lack of information, schools must take fundamental responsibility for education in the broadest sense of the term. For this reason classes in sexual education given in schools should include questions of desire, of pleasure, of respect for one's partner, no matter who that partner is. Sexual education classes should not be limited only to the prevention of AIDS, although it is still an extremely important issue today.

Above and beyond the cultural impoverishment, a ban on casual contact between young women and men in the suburbs outlaws sexuality. And this impasse has led to violence. To charm someone, to build a relationship, you have to be near enough, exchange words in a calm atmosphere. Such conditions have become impossible in the projects, where mixed-sex groups have disappeared. The moral pressure imposed on young women distorts love relationships of any kind. The imperative of virginity weighs heavily on their daily lives, and if they lose it they know they will pay dearly. Any young woman who has slept around gets a bad reputation. Rumors circulate throughout the projects, branding her. She's not a "good girl" any more but an easy woman; she's called a "bitch" and treated as such. The guys in the project can do anything they like with her.

In the scheme of relations just described, love affairs can only be lopsided, full of anxiety and prejudice. What should be a natural and spontaneous relationship becomes an offense, a "sin" liable to draw a penalty from the court of neighborhood opinion. As a bonus, rejection by others and the threat of divine sanctions! Love relationships do not thrive in the projects. Nor are they simple, according to the young men. A boy in love—called a *quécro*—is like a *bouffon* (gay), as far as his pals are concerned, and so he will do everything he can to hide his love from them. In the macho world, feelings are a sign of weakness; only manly values matter. A young man in love could be tender with his girlfriend in private and treat her like dirt in public. For a young woman who is dating a gang member, life can quickly become hell because the others always get involved.

In one-on-one discussions with young men I watched the transformation. Away from the guys, they know how to be calm, tender, and attentive. Some of them can make extraordinary statements, recite poetry, write letters as if they were Alfred de Musset in the suburbs! But the moment their pals join them, they change completely. Their language and attitude toward women immediately shift to violence. When young men are in a group, aggression surfaces. A boy will avoid dating his friends' sisters because relationships like that would be seen as treason. Once in a while there are Romeo and Juliet romances in the projects; a girl and a boy from the same neighborhood, who have grown up together, fall in love but cannot go on because you can't do that to your buddy.

To show how well they conform to the macho model, young men play at being tough and boast of "laying their girlfriend." Of course some do not share the model, but to keep the peace they go along. A flirtation never lasts very long. The very toughest guys treat women as objects to trade back and forth. Some of them even go so far as to "share" the same girlfriend and set up traps so others in the group will look up to them. These are *tournantes*, a new term for gang rapes, sometimes including acts of brutality. In her book Samira Bellil explains what happens, and we also collected testimony during the march.[1] One tragic case was related by the head teacher at a secondary school. Several years ago two of his students died the same night, a brother and sister. The boy was fifteen, his sister thirteen. "That evening," the teacher explained, "his buddies came to get him at home, they were organizing a gang rape in a hut nearby. They were a gang from another neighborhood, one he hardly knew, but he followed them anyway. When they arrived at the site, the rape had already begun, and the victim was his own sister. So he lost control. He went home, borrowed his father's gun, returned to the site, and shot everyone, killing his sister first, the others next. Then he turned the gun against himself."[2] But let's not hide the truth: group rape is not new, and it does not occur just in the housing projects. It happens in the plush parts of the city, but they talk about it less.

In the suburbs romance is never a simple experience. You never see couples embracing below high-rise buildings. Everyone suffers enormously from this situation. Young people from the projects are starving for love and for attention and respect. You can hear it in the rap culture. At the outset this music and dance,

1. [Trans.] See *Dans l'enfer des tournantes* (2002), for Samira Bellil's account of gang rapes in similar circumstances.
2. Testimony from the *Livre blanc des femmes des quartiers*.

with its macho phrases and gestures, can appear really tough. All the more so in light of a macho shift in the rap culture that tolerates women's presence only in the chorus or in ambiguous clips. But when you listen closely to the words, you realize these kids simply want to be loved; life weighs heavily on their shoulders. Besides, even though young women have a hard time breaking into this milieu, singers like Princesse Aniès, Diam's, and several others are helping rap music move in a good direction, thanks to their artistry.

MANDATORY VIRGINITY AND WAYS AROUND IT

Young women get by as they can, to experience romance. Generally they avoid going out with a young man from the projects and look elsewhere, but the relationship must remain secret. The motto remains "To live happily, live in secret." Any flirtation must remain hidden, and even outside the projects it would be risky to be seen hand-in-hand with a young man.

At Solidarity House we have heard many accounts to this effect. Stories of brothers who settle up with the boy, then rough up their sister. Then the father gets a certificate of virginity to verify that the young woman has not lapsed. Such stories seem like ancient history, but they constitute a bitter present-day reality. In our neighborhoods today there are doctors who specialize in certificates of virginity. Some are merely obliging, but most of them maintain this practice because they know that false virginity certificates are the only means of saving young women from possibly terrible acts of revenge. Such verification is not enough to let a girl off completely. She must pay, and so must her mother, who was responsible for watching over her. The young woman is beaten, confined to the home, and sometimes sent back to the village or forced into marriage. The men of the family do everything they can to save the family's honor and their name. Punishment can go as far as murder.

Mandatory virginity kills young women in the projects—both literally and figuratively—because it also destroys all freedom. The hymen has become the symbol of a private body that guards the honor of the family and the community. Young men have taken control over women's bodies and they have become their jailers. Women who are children of immigrants are not the only ones concerned. The statements we collected during our march for equality revealed that young French women are experiencing the same treatment as their immigrant friends. While they live with their family they can perhaps discuss issues of sexuality and their relationships with young men, but once the young French women leave home, their freedom is over. Once they cross that threshold, they experience the same violence others do. They are observed and policed in the same way by men and by the court of neighborhood opinion. Condemnation would be equally brutal if news got out that they had had sexual relations.

HIDDEN SEXUALITY

Living with oppression has profoundly changed women's romantic and sexual experience. A genuine regression to the past has brought back macho behavior to relations within couples. A new moral order exists and has taken women hostage. It has not prevented sexual relations—many young women, whether they wear the headscarf or not, have sex—but imposes certain limits.

Because they must remain virgins in order to preserve the family honor, these young women agree to hidden sexuality, which unfortunately often means sodomy, especially the first time they have sex. When I use the word "unfortunately," it carries no moral judgment but reflects their unhappy experience. All the testimony collected in the working paper drafted for the estates general showed this to be true.

It is very hard to listen to a young woman of sixteen or seventeen, very much in love with her boyfriend, tell us her fears that he will leave her if she does not make love with him. Life in the projects is full of such contradictions. Most of the girls agree to have sex on condition that they preserve their virginity and are regularly sodomized. In their words they feel no pleasure from this limited type of sexual relation, and they give in only to satisfy their boyfriend's desire.

They submit to conform to a model—remain a virgin until marriage—and to satisfy male desire. But deprived of any pleasure, such relationships quickly become unbearable. When they manage to talk about it in confidence, they are in tears. And the refrain we hear behind their words is unspeakable: they cannot live with their virginity, and without it they are nothing.

Hardest of all, they know that giving in will not stop the young man from leaving them. Romantic love, particularly in adolescence, is always painful, but for these young women, the fact of being abandoned seems all the more brutal because they have the impression of having given as much of themselves as is permissible and bearable. They tell themselves that they have given everything and that, in the end, it does not matter to boys. So many of these girls marry at an increasingly early age, at seventeen or eighteen, in the hope that they will have more freedom in leaving the family circle. But they escape from one constraint only to find themselves faced with another: they come back, often at twenty-one or twenty-two, divorced and with a child that they are now raising alone.

The gap between my generation and theirs appears staggering to me. We fought for the right to live our own sexuality. Although the subject was taboo, our families tacitly accepted the relationships we had with our boyfriends. Everyone knew, but it was one of those things we left unsaid.

5

From Neighborhood to Ghetto

More and more, I sense, our suburbs are in a cycle of advanced social and political breakdown. The phenomenon is not new, but it has grown with the economic crisis of the 1990s.

ABANDONED BY THE STATE

This drift reflects the growing poverty in our neighborhoods as the economic recovery of the mid-1990s bypassed the suburbs. Even as unemployment decreased and the French saw their purchasing power increase, the inhabitants of the projects remained outside the system and became further entrenched in poverty. Those who managed to pull through quickly got out. Often these were French families, and the successive waves of immigrants came first from the Maghreb, then Turkey, and Africa in the last years. Instead of reacting to this situation, the government continued its policies of social segregation, thus aggravating the poverty in these neighborhoods. Both the mayors and the office of low-cost housing gave up any attempt to encourage the mixing of social classes in the suburbs and to push it in particular for the housing projects.[1] And, of course, there were serious consequences to such neglect! Segregation, confinement, poverty, dilapidation of property, departures of those who could afford to do so—on and on, in a vicious circle.

The inhabitants' impression of confinement increased with the decline of popular education programs. As the associative movement entered its crisis, public authorities simultaneously and systematically reduced the numbers of social workers in the neighborhoods. The difference between the period of my youth and the present is striking. Yet I too was born in a neighborhood composed of nearly 90 percent Algerian immigrants and 10 percent European families, who all got along without problems. Children were raised with strict discipline and with respect for adults. Our housing projects also had some public infrastructure, popular education, and youth clubs under the patronage of local associations; the young people of my generation had access to such activities and we were looked after and supervised. The youth workers who were physically present in the streets of the projects did a great job and even came to meet our families. And then, after the election of François Mitterand as president in

1. [Trans.] After World War I and into the 1930s the government built *habitations à loyers modérés* (low-cost housing), in attempts to improve working-class housing. Many of the building projects of the 1960s and 1970s experimented with satellite towns in the Paris region and cement high-rise construction in existing suburbs to house immigrant workers but rarely linked the suburbs adequately to the city centers.

1981, immigrants were able to create a large number of associations of their own.[2] The spurt in growth of the associative movement allowed for the development of cultural activities in the projects, helping strengthen social cohesion there by facilitating integration in the republic.

But little by little, the state reduced the number of youth workers, put an end to public service in certain projects, and withdrew from the neighborhoods. As for the associations, they had to jump hurdles to get financing because the applications became more complex and the delays before payment was made were very long. As a result, through lack of real support, many neighborhood associations went under. The militants and the inhabitants of these neighborhoods, watching the situation decline, alerted the local and national authorities, but the latter did not have the political will to seek the human and financial means necessary to counteract this breakdown. Even so, the opportunity was there: to stop discriminatory practices in housing, to renew social and ethnic mixing in the projects, and to rebuild social ties by setting up jobs for youth workers. But—aside from a few measures they took in the context of town policies that had little effect on the inhabitants of the projects—political authorities did not measure the scale of the work to be done. For some time several organizations and associations had been asking for a "Marshall plan" for the neighborhoods, to

2. [Trans.] In 1981 the Socialist government of François Mitterand granted equal rights of association to France's foreign population—giving impetus to ethnic minority cultural associations—by abrogating a 1939 law that required foreigners to obtain authorization from the minister of the interior to form any association.

make a real change for their inhabitants, and to settle once and for all what was euphemistically called at the time "the malaise of the suburbs." But these signals of alarm went unheard.

NEIGHBORHOOD BOYS, BETWEEN BITTERNESS AND PRAGMATISM

As the suburbs drifted downward, the language used to describe their status changed. In the 1980s, one spoke of "malaise"; today it is called decline and ghettoization. This is a sign of profound change, easy to pick up in the language of young people. The suburbs became a social and cultural wasteland as unemployment among young men in the neighborhoods increased. Economic recovery left the suburbs behind. This exclusion from the national economic upswing solidified the sense of rejection, underlining the republic's perceived unwillingness to integrate all its children. A great majority of the young men from the projects experienced a dramatic, immense sense of injustice and rejection by French society (young women, of course, had been struggling since childhood).

In all the discussions I had with young men, particularly those between the ages of eleven and twenty-five, I heard the same nagging refrain. They consider that they have been "parked" in the projects. In their view the political authorities on both the Left and the Right have abandoned them. So for survival some of them organize on their own. They explain very simply how some of them have been thrown into parallel economies within the projects, the only means of obtaining easy money, of having a social role, and of existing. Make no mistake: the parallel economy clearly offers social recognition to people who have no other norms than the law of silence, the law of the strongest. Kids admire these guys who deal in various goods (drugs, clothing, or larger appliances that have "fallen off trucks," as they say) and bring home cash. It's not surprising that films such as *The Godfather* or *Scarface* have become cult films for them, just as for the young men in American ghettos.

Young people of this third generation have critically assessed the results of our struggles as militants in the Beur movement of the 1980s. For a long time we represented an example for them to follow. But today they judge us harshly. I've been in numerous meetings where they implied that, certainly we had struggled, demanded our rights, but in return the politicians spoke only of our duties and, in particular, our duty to integrate. And they find themselves up against the same admonition to comply, even though they were born here, sometimes of parents with French nationality! They think we fought for very little and got almost nothing. In their view the patent proof of this failure is our absence from public political life. They criticize our presence on municipal electoral lists as token figures like blacks, Rebeus, and Beurettes[3]—and especially our inability to get any job among the decision makers, with enough power to fix the misdeal. It is hard to hear this criticism, but they are not all wrong, even if I think that today attitudes are changing and evolving in the right direction. We shall see.

3. [Trans.] For municipal elections in 2001 several cities solicited candidates from ethnic minorities, but many such candidates avoided labels, identifying themselves as citizens, mothers, or heads of households, hoping to avoid co-optation. See Malika Ghemmaz, "Les candidats d'origine maghrébine face au risque d'instrumentalisation," *Hommes et migrations* 1243 (May–June 2003): 65–77.

Their approach to life is much more cynical, pragmatic, perhaps more realistic than ours was. This third generation was born into a tough and difficult context of mass unemployment that has left traces on their families. In some way they are a generation that has been sacrificed and is incapable of planning for the future and holding up an ideal for society. This assessment is of course valid for young people everywhere. But in the projects its impact magnifies the phenomenon of their depolitization and makes it more important and profound. Young people have only one goal in mind, making money, and only one means to exist, power relations and violence.

To get by and to be respected in the neighborhoods, you have to show signs of wealth: having money has become the new norm. For our generation, as I said, the notions of solidarity, of respect—the values our parents transmitted to us—counted enormously. During my youth, for example, it was impossible to imagine lacking respect for your father or mother. In particular, a mother was untouchable: she had given birth, raised, and, in the collective imagination, sacrificed a great deal for her children's education. Today, this myth is shopworn. Some young people of this third generation do not respect their mother and think it's all nonsense. And when you bring down this symbol, so crucially important to us, the rest of life takes on little importance. All moral references explode. No surprise that they next show little respect for their own sisters or, more generally, for women in the projects.

The current process of ghettoization and its consequences for young men's behavior resembles in a strange way what happened in the United States. And so I use the term *ghetto* knowingly, as it is ordinarily used to describe a situation proper to the United

States, because the same ingredients feed into the process of breakdown in the French suburbs. In these neighborhoods we find the same poverty and the same social destitution. Parked in poor neighborhoods, abandoned by politicians, young people have turned to trafficking of all kinds, in a parallel economy, and invoke only one means of expression, violence, with its settling of scores, its gangs. Many young people think their lives are over. They no longer believe in a system that continues to exclude them. They cannot imagine the future, so they operate in the immediate present. When I hear these young men explain to me that they are organizing among themselves because they do not want anything to do with a society that has excluded them, that there is no reason to fight to participate in a society that rejects them, I tell myself that we are losing the battle for republican integration. And we are ruining the lives of kids who create their own universe far from the framework of the republic. To be sure, they represent a minority in our neighborhoods. But they poison life there by imposing their model. Other young men who do not play their game keep quiet.

Thus we see only this delinquent minority. Yet many young men, children of immigrants, made their way out of the projects. For them, integration and social mobility worked. And young men like these could become leaders, could become elite examples to show the way. But in order to do this, they have to make themselves visible or return to the projects. It takes courage to come back and share responsibility for the little sisters and brothers left behind who would like things to change.

Many years have passed, but nothing has happened to change the world young people in the suburbs see around them. They have seen neglect and inaction settle in and people remain parked where they are. Within this situation of confinement a Mafia-like system has emerged with its own social norms and codes of behavior, heightening the sense of insecurity we heard so much about during the last presidential campaign. Yet it warrants another hearing in this context, because, after all, the first victims were indeed all those people living in the projects as hostages to their activist minority.

FROM NEIGHBORHOODS TO GHETTOS

This decline began much earlier than the march in the Minguettes suburb of Lyon in the 1980s, though reports claim otherwise. It began as the first immigrants and then the *pieds-noirs* arrived en masse in France.[4] They were put into makeshift housing, in "transit" cities (as they were notoriously called) that were supposed to be only temporary. In fact, these slums lasted for decades and nothing was done to get rid of them. Things got fixed up, of course, but the policy intended only to cover up the worst conditions. Public authorities adopted a strategy of doing nothing with the idea that foreigners would inevitably return home. But people remained and the slums in which they lived became neighborhoods. Despite the constant public proclamation of attachment to republican values and to equality, there was never a show of real political will to transform this housing. These people were treated in a slipshod way. If there had ever been real political will, the ghettos would not exist today.

4. [Trans.] The first immigrants Amara mentions came before and after World War I. The *pieds-noirs* were French settlers in Algeria who came back to live in France during and after the Algerian War.

The Mafia-like organizations identified in recent years really do exist in the neighborhoods. They consist of young people organized in gangs with leaders and underlings. Today you see kids of ten and twelve who are paid a commission for watching for the police patrol and informing those who are dealing further down the street. How can you explain to them afterward about the value of real work? How do you remind them that they need to go to school to get a diploma and find a job? This is the terrible day-to-day reality of the projects today. It is deceptive to judge public housing neighborhoods by their facade. As Harlem Désir said in 1985, "It's not enough to repaint the stairwells."[5] To be sure, renovating the habitat is a necessary policy step, but the human element cannot be ignored. Despite the repainting, the ghetto was created and it has become rooted in neighborhood inhabitants' heads.

Today there is great concern for the situation of young Muslim women. But it masks larger socioeconomic problems. Isolation and violence have settled in our neighborhoods and their first victims are the inhabitants. My comparison with American ghettos may seem exaggerated and excessive if you look only at the visual and the built environment. But when you take the time to really observe what is happening in our suburbs, you see the same degradation. The scale is different because American ghettos stand for entire cities. Since the same causes yield the same effects, now is the time to act and stop this escalation.

5. [Trans.] Harlem Désir, then the well-respected director of SOS Racisme, helped publicize the antiracism campaign through the yellow badge "Touche pas à mon pote."

6

Obscurantism, the Key to Regression

Reference is often made in France to "basement Islam." To understand this expression, which today designates the shadowy Islam of religious obscurantism, you need to know that it once referred to an Islam of impartiality and forgiveness, now slowly emerging within the French Republic. The beautifully constructed Paris mosque, dating from 1928, demonstrates that progress is still possible when the will exists and all actors agree. I discovered the magnificence of this building during a conversation with Dalil Boubakeur, the rector of the Paris mosque, after the march.[1] Like every other visitor, I was charmed by the atmosphere of serenity. The experience was even more memorable because my talk with the rector was cordial and productive. Dalil Boubakeur assured us of his total support and encouraged us in the campaign we were undertaking.

1. [Trans.] Boubakeur represents a moderate current among the several religious organizations claiming to speak for Islam in France.

THE EMERGENCE OF A NEW POLITICAL ISLAM

Without money or places to worship, the first immigrants set up prayer rooms wherever they could. Often such places were vacant rooms or even basements the managers of the housing projects let them use. Sometimes the Catholic Church loaned a room to the Muslim community, which was the case for the mosque in Clermont-Ferrand. And in my view, we should have encouraged similar arrangements elsewhere, if only to promote a dialogue between religions. These prayer rooms where our parents gathered were also places of sociability. In fact, after prayers people got together to talk and often found that, collectively, they could resolve a family's problems. Solidarity was rife during this period, and the major concern of all parents in these neighborhoods was their children's success in school. I remember that when one of us got a diploma, the whole neighborhood proudly celebrated the event. Madame Dufraisse, who had lived in our neighborhood since it was built, always showed up with chocolate bars she distributed to students like merit points. And when anyone, male or female, went on to the university, it was a victory we could make our own, even as kids. During this period, studying at the university was very desirable but nevertheless reserved for a certain elite, and we felt real joy when someone in our neighborhood succeeded. I remember one proud and happy father—a construction worker nicknamed "broken arm" because of an accident on the job—because his daughter, Yasmina, obtained her baccalaureate and continued her studies at university that eventually landed her in the United States. Today she continues her brilliant career in a large French company. Her father, like so many others, had made sacrifices in order to offer his children a better future. This was the environment in which I lived until the late 1980s, when nearly everyone lost their jobs and our suburbs began to drift. Little by little every landmark, every levee gave way. And in this social emptiness obscurantism took root.

Thus in the 1990s fundamentalist Islam came onto the scene. It had developed in the wake of the Muslim Brotherhood, bringing with it misinterpretations of the Koran and, as if by chance, misreadings of sacred texts on the status of women.[2] In France in particular, its reactionary preachers—known as "basement imams"—developed a very macho political discourse on confining the individual. The context helps explain how basement Islam could spread and exercise such an influence over the neighborhoods: it emerged when a significant number of young people from the projects were completely disoriented, facing failure in school, unemployment, and discrimination. They all carried the suburbs' stigma and the impression they could never leave it behind. In the search for personal identity, militant Islam was one of the few answers they found. At the outset everyone felt reassured that they had found a new framework for their lives, one that broke with the pattern of worshiping money and trafficking. Islam had become a new governing moral system to keep idle young people from turning to delinquency. Thus by 1995 in some areas the local authorities and elected representatives across the political spectrum, and notably the mayors, recognized the

2. [Trans.] The Muslim Brotherhood began in 1928 in Egypt as a revivalist movement, tinged with nationalism, that advocated a return to a purified Islam as a defense against British colonialism and Western domination in general.

radical imams and chose them as privileged spokesmen. This was a terrible blow for the militants of my generation, who never asked religious authorities to intervene in public affairs. We knew the danger that such intervention could entail in a general way, but particularly in relation to young women. The danger applies to all religious extremists, of whatever faith. Suddenly all of us activists who had used the language of universalism to militate in favor of individual rights, regardless of sex, found ourselves marginalized in the life of the projects.[3] The political authorities no longer referred to us or recognized us as potential spokespersons for the projects; we were just troublemakers who were fighting the imams' influence. From that moment, whenever there was a problem in the projects, it was no longer the youth worker or the neighborhood coordinator or the associations' militants who were asked to resolve it, but the local imam.

The authorities began to treat directly with these religious men or with young people they held in their sway; these were new leaders of public opinion, people you could talk to. The imam turned himself into the new social regulator. Outside recognition had reinforced his authority within the projects. Parents believed it was good for young people to go to prayers rather than hang around the projects and look for fights. But these religious men did not profess the calm Islam of tolerance practiced by our parents. The harmful influence of basement Islam drove members of some families apart. Disagreements

3. [Trans.] Amara's reference to "the language of universalism" puts her firmly within the tradition of the French Republic and its values and also within a strand of French equal rights feminism from the nineteenth and early twentieth centuries (women won the right to vote in 1945).

broke out between the parents, on the one side, who had little understanding of this radical and dangerous practice, and the children, on the other, who criticized their parents for "ignorance," because of their illiteracy and their lack of rigorous knowledge of the Koran.

Basement Islam drew on factors such as unemployment, the ghettoization of the projects, the retreat into sectarian politics—with racist and anti-Semitic undertones—and feelings of discrimination and injustice. Through its religious propagation of intolerance basement Islam offered young men a theoretical framework and tools with which to oppress young women. If young women did not fit the mold, they were "heathens" or "women of bad reputation." These far from random terms reveal the power of religious rhetoric. Its influence is much more important than is recognized.

From the moment imams settled into a number of projects, some of the young men began to apply radical codes of behavior to young women, in particular by forcing them back into their homes. The battle for *mixité*—mixed-sex company—then lost ground. The activist minority that developed around basement Islam has publishing houses, relay stations here and there, intellectuals, and advertising agencies. Nothing is left to chance. Its advocates have even been able to find support from legal decisions, such as the recent Conseil d'Etat decree concerning the headscarf.[4] Or, from another example, the recent decision that

---

4. [Trans.] In 1989 the Conseil d'Etat ruled that wearing religious symbols in public schools was compatible with secularism and thus legal, if it did not intrude on others' rights to religious freedom or in any way entail proselytism.

wearing the headscarf at work is not incompatible with the job. Though according to another ruling, wearing Bermuda shorts to work *is* inappropriate.

The complex issues at stake here raise questions in my mind. Moreover, other activist minorities are gathering their forces, calling for moral renewal on an international level. Here in France, there are fundamentalist Catholic brigades who intervene to stop abortions, while Jewish and Muslim cultural associations demand special bathing hours for public swimming pools, and that is not the end. The republic is being tested on all fronts to resist religious inroads.

THE HEADSCARF AS SYMBOL OF WOMEN'S OPPRESSION

The headscarf is the most visible and telling evidence of this lapse into obscurantism. When the phenomenon first appeared in the late 1980s, with tensions at school over a handful of girls wearing the headscarf, I was among those who said that these young women should not be excluded. Our reasoning was simple: these young women were under pressure from their families; to help them resolve it, it was preferable to keep them at school. We were counting on the republican school system, where they would learn to make their own choice and then to refuse the headscarf. The Conseil d'Etat's decision in 1989, authorizing religious symbols at school on the condition that they not be ostentatious or in any way appear to proselytize, seemed to us a just and balanced decision. It would allow these young women, despite the pressure, to continue to attend school and hence to emancipate themselves. Unfortunately, ten years later the policy has proved a failure. For the French school system has not equipped them with the tools to define themselves within the common secular space we share, each with our own beliefs.

We need to return to the legal texts and apply the ban against religious symbols in the public sphere such as the school. For me, secularism has always meant the freedom to practice my religion within a framework that respects the republic and its values and, obviously, within an appropriate setting. And young people need to understand that the struggle for a secular republic, which began with the French Revolution and continues today, has been hard; some gave up their lives so that others could live with respect. The state, guarantor of secularism, must protect its fundamental values and responsibilities at school and elsewhere. Thanks to two memoranda in 1989 that established the framework for religious practice within the national education system (memoranda from Prime Minister Lionel Jospin and from the minister of education, François Bayrou), the texts already exist. But guarantees must apply to all public services, as spaces that should remain neutral. All of us, whether religiously observant or not, should respect them.

Our reaffirmation of secularism need not be in the form of a law; I think it would be unwise to lay down more rules on such a sensitive topic.[5] I'm counting on people's intelligence: in order to convince people, you need to exchange views, discuss the issues. Otherwise, you run the risk of radicalizing one side or the other. It is equally important not to focus public opinion on the single

5. [Trans.] Fadela Amara revised her position on a law banning the headscarf once the law was passed in March 2004. See the postscript.

issue of the headscarf at the expense of other problems, social ones in particular. For some, wearing a headscarf is a new political argument for stigmatizing Muslims and the suburbs. Those advocates of a new law on secularism fail to realize the impact it will have in our projects. Young people may react violently. Because a law will involve Islam, they are going to feel that once again they have been targeted, and they will take it as further proof that French society has no use for citizens like them. And probably then certain women will be forced to wear burkas, not just headscarves. Beards will appear as evidence of belonging to a religion that is under attack. The effect will be the reverse of what we hoped for, the peaceful coexistence of different religions within a common secular framework.

Moreover, the headscarf is not simply a religious matter. Remember that it is first of all a means of oppression, of alienation, of discrimination, an instrument of power over women used by men—men do not wear headscarves. We must tell young women that they can be Muslims today without wearing the headscarf. I am a practicing Muslim and I have never worn it, neither have my mother or my grandmother before me. To counteract the rhetoric of imams in the suburbs, we need to listen to the voices of such intellectuals as Malek Chebel and many others.[6] We must remember the women who struggle

---

6. [Trans.] The anthropologist and philosopher Malek Chebel and other young Muslim intellectuals hope to "modernize" Islam and, as a first step, to separate religion from politics. Many of Chebel's books on the history of religion, notably in Arab and Muslim civilization, aim at popularizing Islam in the West (they include the *Dictionnaire amoureux d'Islam, Manifeste pour un Islam des Lumières,* and *L'esprit de sérail: mythes et pratiques sexuels au Maghreb*).

every day in certain Muslim countries—with the support of men who share their fight for freedom—for the right to refuse to wear the headscarf, notably in Algeria, where the price it exacts is steep.

Their voices carry even more urgent meaning because they express Islam as experienced and practiced by the huge "silent" majority. The history of Muslim civilization has taught us how much Islamic culture has contributed to the progress of humanity. Many specialists of various persuasions have written eloquently on the fundamental importance of Muslim sciences, poetry, and art. Muslim societies' considerable refinement strongly influenced Western societies, and it was through this exchange of knowledge between the two cultures that the world evolved. Thus I find it hard to accept the animosity toward Islam that lingers after 11 September 2001. Like many others, I was overcome by this horrible drama and consider it a tragedy for humanity. Obscurantism commits blind murder everywhere in the world and it is imperative to react and combat it. These unspeakable actions affect us all. But should they burden the whole Muslim community? No, assuredly not! Fortunately, the huge majority of men and women committed to justice and freedom have not made the error of implicating all Muslims in their condemnation. Even so, unfortunately, there have been attempts to assign blame.

Hence my surprise when Oriana Fallaci—a renowned journalist and human rights activist—published, in the wake of the terrorist attacks against the United States, a work titled *The Rage and the Pride*, which is nothing more than a blanket condemnation of the entire Muslim community. It was difficult for me to admit that such a woman was capable of such infamy. Oriana

Fallaci has been recognized all over the world for her commitment in the struggle against fascism in Italy, led jointly with her father. For this reason, her charge hurt me all the more. Has this great lady been blinded? However, I find no excuse for it and wrote an open letter to tell her so.

It has always been my position that each of us is responsible for our own actions. As for the controversial headscarf issue, we must truly approach it calmly, dispassionately. To hold onto our sanity, we must remember that the recommendation for women to cover their heads has always caused debate within the Muslim community, ever since the Prophet's death. I am not going to enter into theological discussions on the interpretation of the Koran and its precepts—I have no claim to do so. For my part, I would rather see young women wear the revolutionaries' red cap than the headscarf.[7] I remain convinced that we have the best guarantee of living freely in mutual respect within the framework of a secular republic.

7. [Trans.] Called the *bonnet rouge* (or *phrygien*), the cap appeared in the summer of 1791 as a popular symbol of liberty; in 1792 even Louis XVI was forced to wear it. Freed slaves in ancient Greece first wore the cap, now identified with the republic and visible on various images of Marianne. On its symbolic importance see Jack Censer and Lynn Hunt, *Liberty, Equality, Fraternity: Exploring the French Revolution* (University Park: Pennsylvania State University Press, 2001), 82; and Nicole Pellegrin, *Les vêtements de la liberté* (Aix-en-Provence: Editions Alinéa, 1989), 32.

PART TWO

An Act of Survival

The March and Its Success

7

Preparations for the March

We first sounded the alarm about the increasing violence a
decade ago at Solidarity House. Even in 1994, when I was living
in Clermont-Ferrand, we would discuss the problem each time
we met with the mayor. We knew that if nothing were done to
halt this process, it would lead to disaster: the experience of continuous social violence for everyone in the projects, but especially for the young men, victims of the strongest prejudice. The
media regularly call them an "activist minority" and responsible
for the violence but never note that the majority of young men
in our neighborhoods are trying desperately to survive. Many of
them react negatively and violently to the way others perceive
them. They assume their lives are shot, whatever they do: violence is the only way out—through dominating the weakest
members of the community, who are in the first place young
women.

FIRST STEPS TO HELP WOMEN

In 1989 we created a women's commission at Solidarity House in Clermont-Ferrand. I was named to head it because I knew about the situation of young women in the projects, having lived through it some years earlier. Within the framework of this commission we decided to tackle the problems young women encountered because they had no freedom of movement in the projects. We also dealt with some delicate situations, such as girls running away from home, girls who got pregnant—tough problems at the time, but in fact we were just starting out and things soon got worse. Most of the young women I met during our office hours were girls I had known since they were very little. It was hard to listen to a young girl I had watched grow up explain that she was pregnant, and to see how terrified she was. I was deeply troubled that the associations and the national education administration had not envisaged the problem of sexuality in the projects, in families where nothing got discussed.

What I began to anticipate and found very frightening was the emergence of physical violence. Even without years of study, it was obvious to us that at a given moment violence would flare up. It was not going to stop with bans on going out, or even with insults and clashes. Together with the other members of the women's commission we warned against the pattern of mounting violence but did not know what to do to stop it and lacked the means to fight against it.

So we continued our work for women and girls. We enlisted the help of the municipal government of Clermont-Ferrand and of Michèle André, the secretary of state for women's rights under the Socialist government of Michel Rocard, who heard our pleas, and of the indomitable Michel Charasse, who was always there when we needed him. But at the same time we realized that this aid would not be enough, that we could not act against increasing violence without stopping the process of ghettoization. What was needed was a well-defined and well-funded policy to break down barriers between neighborhoods and integrate their populations socially and ethnically. From the moment in the 1980s when the suburbs had been cited as a problem, and violence had erupted in the Minguettes neighborhood of Lyon, resulting in the Beur March of 1983, we had been convinced that our objective was right. Breaking down the ghettos was the only way to resolve part of the problem of violence. If people had listened to us then, perhaps the situation would not have degenerated to this point.

The first acts of violence against women were hushed up and little was reported, but we had already identified them. There were kidnappings and forced returns to a country of origin, forced marriages, and even murders of young women branded as "ruined." We tried to alert public authorities and political leaders, but no one listened. Then in October 2002 Sohane, an eighteen-year-old woman, was set on fire by a young man in a utility room in a suburban housing project in Vitry-sur-Seine near Paris. His motive—spurned love or a gang conflict—was never clearly established, but the murder produced an electroshock in public opinion. A silent march several days later drew a large crowd of young people from the neighborhoods, to honor Sohane and to urge a halt to the violence. The event also led to the creation in June 2003 of a collective called "Feminine-Masculine" that aimed at promoting respect for women in the projects. Sohane's murder marked a turning point, but we were already aware of other serious incidents and had begun to react.

When I joined the national executive of the Federation of Solidarity Houses in 2000 and became responsible for the women's commission, I lobbied to make women's issues one of our national campaigns. Moreover, in December that year I was elected president of the federation with a project to focus our work almost exclusively on women. I was convinced that making women's issues a priority would involve us in every facet of the suburban malaise. Women's issues would give us a political framework. Rather than discuss malaise as an abstraction, loosely defined and irrational, we would talk about individuals, young women in a situation of extreme distress. We had already explored the approach with Malek Boutih when he was president of SOS Racisme; he was one of the first people to offer his active support. There was public concern for women's issues, we realized, beyond our work to strengthen social cohesion and integration within the republic. Thus from 2000 on we began to set up women's commissions within Solidarity Houses and their affiliated associations across the nation.

Because the commissions had various activities and limited time, I felt we should take stronger measures. So we decided to organize a training seminar on the history of feminism for neighborhood women. We could not carry out our campaign if those most concerned, the women and girls in the projects, had little understanding of our goals. The stakes were high, because women in the projects wanted nothing to do with the feminist movement. For them, feminism was senseless. To speak about the right to choose your life, about contraception, about financial independence in these neighborhoods seemed crazy.

Yet they desperately needed to know about feminists' past struggles, and, in fact, to appropriate them for themselves. In June 2000 we held a training seminar on feminism at the Federation of Solidarity Houses in Paris; we had prepared a dossier of some four hundred pages that traced the history of feminism, from the suffragettes to the demonstrations and petitions in favor of abortion, and touched on the struggles in the United States. The seminar was a great success; eighty people from all over France, from all generations and geographic origins, women and men, participated. We then realized how strong the interest was, because we had never had such strong attendance at one of our meetings. Moreover, we had never had so many reactions and questions during our organized debates. For our militants, the history of feminist struggles was a real discovery.

THE ESTATES GENERAL
OF NEIGHBORHOOD WOMEN

In response and as follow-up to comments and debates during the seminar, we worked throughout 2001 to prepare the Estates General of Neighborhood Women. At the same time we continued our regular federation activities (neighborhood meals, international solidarity workshops, Christmas tree parties, etc.). Thus in fall 2001 we organized local estates general that were, in fact, public meetings throughout the country, in cities such as Strasbourg, Narbonne, Clermont-Ferrand, Lille, Bordeaux, Marseille, as well as in many towns in the Paris region. The first objective was to have all young women realize that they were not isolated individuals, that the situation they were experiencing was happening in all the suburbs. I spent my time crisscrossing the Paris region and the provinces to convince my co-workers and to organize the local estates general. We relied on our own networks that were also open to other associations. Many of them, such as Planned Parenthood, picked up immediately on our approach and came to participate in our collective preparatory meetings for the local estates general. We met with them to stimulate debates, to explain the way we understood things, why this situation had emerged, and how we might try to alert public opinion and thus reach public authorities. We had to convince our public that it was possible to create a powerful force to turn the situation around in the projects, notably for young women. The local estates general played an essential role in this consciousness-raising. Later, during the march in 2003, we observed a freedom of expression that was the fruit of more than two and a half years of work.

We went back to a number of towns where we had organized public meetings, at the request of young women. Clearly, the meetings answered a real need. Women appropriated our approach and were able to move forward thanks to the dynamic it created; they plunged into collective work. This was already a first sign of victory because, as we knew, the best thing that could happen in the projects to counteract the older brothers' authority would be to break the law of silence, to give girls and boys who were in difficulty and who were victims of these codes of masculine behavior a chance to express themselves. It would be a great step forward just to say "Stop, that's enough. This is what I am living and what I see in my project. I've had enough." You have to understand that the notorious activist minority had easily won the battle, because it had taken over the whole project with little or no resistance.

During the sequence of local estates general and in preparation for one at the national level, we sent out a questionnaire that targeted specific problems such as violence, sexuality, traditions, and religion. We received over five thousand responses. The sociologist Helen Orain put together a working paper (*Livre blanc des femmes des quartiers*) with this material, based on young women's testimony of their personal experiences. The paper confirmed our analysis of what had been happening in the projects: mounting violence, social breakdown, ghettoization, retreat into sectarian politics, ethnic and sexual discrimination, the powerful return to tradition, the weight of myth about virginity, but also practices like excision and polygamy still current in certain African communities.

The Estates General of Women from the Neighborhoods met from 26 to 27 January 2002 at the University of Paris–La Sorbonne. Only women had been invited because many young women had told us at the local estates general, "It is difficult for us to speak when there are young men present." Thus we decided that the national meeting would be closed to men. The three hundred women who attended—a blending of geographic origins and generations, and ages ranging from fifteen to over fifty years old—included our mothers as well, because a dialogue across generations was essential. The program provided four themes for discussion: sexuality, the weight of tradition and religion (does it handicap women's emancipation?), professional training, and access to jobs. All of a sudden, as the discussions progressed, we could feel the taboos fall away and the tongues relax. Without the male gaze to judge them, young women dared to expose what they had been experiencing. They talked about how they would dress in huge sweaters in order to cross the projects and then take them off when they reached school; the detours they would take to avoid the gangs of boys on their path;

the difficulty of going out alone and the obligation to travel with groups of other young women for fear of attacks; their general confinement and the limitations on their going out; their limited access to sports and cultural activities; the tensions and aggression in their relations with boys; the impossibility of happy love relationships. At emotionally charged moments during the meetings these three hundred women, realizing that they had experienced the same violence, announced that they had had enough and wanted to change their lives.

THE MANIFESTO OF NI PUTES NI SOUMISES

After the national estates general, we published an appeal in March 2002, signed "Ni Putes Ni Soumises!" It took the form of a national petition (see the text in appendix 1). Our signature resulted from long debate over a slogan that would be striking, that would sensitize public opinion and political leaders, and that would especially open the eyes of millions of young women. The expression "all whores except my mother" seemed to us to best illustrate the way men considered women in the neighborhoods. No, we were not whores, but neither were we the submissive women described by the outside world. We had heard often enough that if women in the projects were so badly treated, it was because they never revolted. Hence we chose the name Ni Putes Ni Soumises. It bothered some people but was certainly effective.

Some prostitutes wrote to protest that they felt our slogan stigmatized them. Their letter took us by surprise because we had never thought about prostitution in literal terms when we chose the name. It was far from our intention to stigmatize prostitutes;

on the contrary, we felt total solidarity with these women. So many girls fell into prostitution in the projects! Just the opposite reaction came from other prostitutes, who contacted us through the association Bus des femmes (women's bus) to show their support for our decision.[1] Our meeting with this group was very moving, for these women have terrible lives but wanted to mark their solidarity with us.

Our manifesto of demands went to all the candidates in the presidential elections of April 2002.[2] To our great disappointment we received very little response. Almost all the candidates rambled on about insecurity, about the zones of lawlessness in the suburbs, but they never took the trouble to consider the causes or to pay attention to the most obvious victims, the young women in the projects. The political climate was abominable: at the time television carried a continuous stream of alarming news about the housing projects, stigmatizing the young people who

1. [Trans.] The association Bus des femmes was organized to aid the growing numbers of prostitutes in the Paris region, many of them foreigners and victims of sexual tourism. The bus circulates in the evenings to offer them food, medical aid, contraception, and psychological support.

2. [Trans.] The presidential elections of April and May 2002 presented an unusual situation: ten candidates across the political spectrum challenged the incumbent president, Jacques Chirac, who was running for a second seven-year term. After much debate during the campaign over insecurity in the suburbs, in the first round of voting Lionel Jospin, the Socialist Party candidate, was eliminated, and in the second round Chirac faced off against Jean-Marie Le Pen, the Far Right leader of the Front national; its anti-immigration platform pledged to save France for the French. The republican electorate rallied behind Chirac, who won by a large majority.

lived there, the blacks and the Rebeus who hung around there. Some of the media played a very negative role in stirring up an atmosphere of hysteria about young people, and not just any young people, but those in the projects.

Another frightening incident that took place on 20 April 2002 in Orléans, just on the eve of the elections, deserves mention— the attack against "Papy Voise," a seventy-two-year-old who was mugged in his home and saw his house set on fire because the young hoodlums who attacked him couldn't find his savings. Images of his swollen face as he lay in a hospital bed appeared on all the news programs. Viewing this horrible and revolting drama and noting the general unrest, I had one fear, that this attack had been committed by immigrant youth. In the end, I learned, this was not the case.

Young men from the projects were the targets of such hatred that I wondered what was going to happen. It was incredible, staggering: everyone was talking about us, the people living in the projects, but no one was listening to us! We had the impression that all this fury was orchestrated by people who judged and condemned us but had never set foot in the suburbs. Nonetheless, we made up our mind that this time the debate would not take place without us. We had to make people aware that the inhabitants of the projects were determined to change the existing order so that everyone could live normally, determined to stop the stigmatizing and demonizing of our neighborhoods, all the while making outsiders understand that daily life there was terrible.

We wanted average French people to understand that if their own children had grown up in the conditions that we faced, they would most likely have lost control just as all the violent kids do

today, victims of their social environment. The young are not
born delinquent, but they become so. Delinquency is not
inscribed in your genes, as the Far Right implies, thus profiting
from poverty and suffering.

WHAT IS TO BE DONE? MARCH!

It was at this moment that the idea of organizing a march came
into my head. Since the only way to be heard was to yell, we
would put together an unusual initiative to alert public opinion
and political leaders. A march was the obvious choice. I had
reread Gandhi and Martin Luther King and I wanted a peaceful
march that would involve young people from the projects.
Obviously it had to be mixed-sex, because showing ourselves as
wanting to stir up a war of the sexes was out of the question. The
proposal set off a lively discussion among the members of our
group because several of them were very frightened at the outset
that we would never succeed. I quoted a phrase from François
Mitterand that rang true: "Nothing triumphs over human will."
I was convinced that we could succeed, impelled by the suffering
we had experienced and by the testimony of all the young women
who had come to us to recount their pain. Their words deserved
our respect and could carry us forward. In this way we began
preparation for the march in September 2002.

It was a long and difficult process because we had to convince
our own network of associations. We had to explain that we were
not repeating the Beur March, an event perceived as ethnic
because its organizers were young men of North African origins.
Our plan was to speak in the name of the entire population of the
projects. To be sure, the young women were the first concerned,

but we did not want to limit our approach to only one group. The idea was to start with the issue of the ghetto, what was happening inside, its economic problems, and so on. Problems in the ghetto explain how in a way we became a social movement. Anyway, at the outset many activists had their doubts about the march; they had spent years in the projects patching and mending the social fabric that kept unraveling, and some of them had even given up and no longer believed collective action was possible. They imagined our act as a drop in the ocean. We had to stir them up and get them moving. In contrast, Malek Boutih immediately understood the stakes and told me "Go for it!" He had agonized over the violence against young women in the projects for a long time, and he knew that it was easier for a woman to take on such a project than for a man. The aid from SOS Racisme was crucial to us; its members have experience and a network of relations we still lack. As for the young women in our association, they believed in it from the start and threw themselves into it immediately. And then we found that former militants returned or new ones joined us when we began to work on women's issues. Many associations contacted us to participate in our project.

The preparation for the march was laborious work. We had to choose the stopovers in towns where we already had a militant support group, or in places where associations could act as the relay; we had to discuss with our activists to learn which ones were ready to try this adventure; we had to find lodging and a rental car at each stop. We asked private companies to help, and the group Accor agreed to offer us meals and lodging, for which we were very grateful. Thus, little by little, we were able to organize the twenty-three stops on the march, and as the weeks passed we saw young women move forward and young men begin to ask questions. I was eager to have them participate, because I have six brothers and I know that some men experience exactly what we do—especially the gays, who are more fragile and who, because they refuse to buy into the law of the strongest, feel its effects. It was important for me to convince them that we had the right approach and that they themselves should participate. I believe we succeeded.

8

The Success of the March

On 1 February 2003 eight of us, six women and two men—
Loubna, Safia, Chrystelle, Ingrid, Nadia, Olivier, Farid, and
myself—set out from Vitry-sur-Seine to honor Sohane, who
had been burned alive there several months earlier. We felt it
was important to link the March by Neighborhood Women for
Equality and against the Ghetto to the tragedy that had shocked
the public into a first sign of awareness about the conditions we
were exposing. In a similar way Samira's testimony of her lived
experience also triggered a reaction. Those who read her
account had been scandalized, even horrified, wondering how it
was possible in France, in a nearby neighborhood, in our modern
society, that a young woman could live through such torture and
barbarism. Group rapes were not a new phenomenon, but for
the first time a victim had the courage to denounce these acts in
a strong voice. In the names of Sohane and Samira we set out on
the march in a climate that seemed inauspicious.

UNEXPECTED SUCCESS

In quick succession many people marked their support by merging with the march at the stopovers. For five weeks the marchers had to follow a tight schedule: early rising, press conference, meeting with the mayor in the town where we were welcomed, meetings with the local associations, lunches organized by women in the projects, visits to several neighborhoods, and after dinner, a public debate or meeting. In each of the twenty-three towns we visited we held discussions and meetings from nine in the morning to three the next morning. The evening debates drew crowds of never less than two hundred people and sometimes nearly eight hundred. There was always a larger audience than local militants had foreseen, in both small and large towns. In Toulouse, for example, a large city in southwestern France where we had no network, a group of local associations had undertaken the organization of our stopover, with a press conference, meetings in the projects, and a rally followed by a demonstration in the city center. It was unbelievable! The media covered our initiative. At the Paris headquarters of the Federation of Solidarity Houses, our co-workers received dozens of calls daily, and many e-mails and letters from people asking whether the march was coming their way and where they could join up on the road.

From the outset we had evidence of support from numerous persons who expressed admiration for "our courage to speak out." From our viewpoint, ours was not an act of courage but rather an expression of profound exasperation, a simple and obvious desire to say "Stop." But very quickly I perceived that we had struck a nerve. As the march progressed we realized that something extraordinary was happening, overtaking us and taken up again by other women. We understood that we were breaking a taboo, one so strong that our initiative had acquired unexpected scope. The need to speak out was overwhelming!

Our experience of the march was extraordinary because we were able to have such rich exchanges. You must understand that it was entirely new and curious for us to hear good things said about us. We had become so used to living in a power relation— pounding on the table to make ourselves heard—that when we saw grandmothers coming toward us bearing flowers, we could not believe it was happening. We were unaccustomed to such outbursts of sympathy and love, because in the projects, even within families, the slightest sign of affection or of love is frightening!

The march was a novel experience for everyone, especially the young women. In the evening at each stopover we assessed the situation and let go of our accumulated feelings; we were like sponges absorbing the thousand and one accounts of poverty and violence we had heard during the day. All the women in the march were deeply moved by the stories they understood as echoes of their own. Dealing with our emotions on the march was not easy, so that when we reached Paris we were all emotionally drained, but determined.

EMOTIONAL ENCOUNTERS

I remember certain expressions of support that touched me more than others. The first woman who called to encourage me was my mother. She had been frightened by the idea that I could be attacked with acid or assaulted, but she knew that she had never been able to dissuade me from doing something once I had made up my mind. So she called me every day. One day she told me something I will never forget: "When I was your age, if I had been able to do what you are trying to do, I would have done it. When you are marching, it's as if I were marching too." I understood from this that she was proud and that she projected onto me all the struggles she had been unable to undertake. These words were so strong that they sustained me all through the march, even in moments of exhaustion and despondency.

There were also anonymous expressions of support. I remember in Toulouse an eighty-year-old grandmother who came to salute our courage and said to me, "It's extraordinary what you are doing." During our conversation she told me about her life, of her commitment at seventeen to participate in the Resistance alongside the communists, and of her activities during the war. It was difficult for me to understand why she admired us! The comparison with her life experience was incredible, even though our situation in the projects is tough. I was overwhelmed by her support.

Another example, a fourteen-year-old girl from the projects, hypersensitive, rebelling against authority, in crisis at school, who approached me after a meeting, very respectfully, almost as if I were an idol not to be touched, and who said: "Madame, you don't realize what you are doing. In bed at night when I think about what I am going to become, trapped in the housing project, what you are saying gives me strength; I feel I am not entirely alone. You have succeeded, I will too." Afterward we talked several times over the phone, and she told me that she followed the march on television. In talking with her I felt that we had made small victories.

Our biggest success during the march was to convince the most reserved young women to recognize the oppression in their lives. Others fiercely denied what was happening: "We are not at all living what you are denouncing. Our housing project is just great, and we do what we please." Discussion with them was often short, but we did not give up. We asked them whether they could go to the movies when they wanted, flirt with boys, bring their boyfriend home, if they could go out just like their brother and come home late. From their responses we understood that they had unconsciously assimilated traditional norms. They spoke about their fathers' rules and taboos about sex. "We are not allowed to do that! We are duty-bound to be virgins at marriage. If I go out, my father would kill me!" They had learned to bow their heads, doing it so easily that they thought it was by their own choice. For some of them the conditioning was so anchored in their behavior that they could never envisage living any other way. But very often at the end of our debates, these women would come to see us and then, face to face, they would let go, relate their daily experience of banned behavior and bullying, the very system of control we were denouncing. One evening one of these young women came to see me to confess: "I have done so many stupid things that this summer I am to be married in Algeria."

The women and girls whom we met began to ask questions—I know this is true because I have remained in contact with several of them—and to understand the behavior that made them bow their heads. They have since changed their outlook on the world and their lives. In my view it is a far greater victory to have touched the lives of these young women than those who were already convinced of the need for change. This victory represents a sign of hope. These young women will someday become mothers and we will watch the legacy they leave to the next generation.

A PROVOCATIVE SOCIAL MOVEMENT

Of course we also had our detractors. We were reproached for stigmatizing the suburbs by identifying them as ghettos. To be sure, ours was not an easy message to convey because it was critical of political leaders both on the Left and the Right, and of all the governments, one after another. And it forced people to look at a reality they have ignored for a long time. But I sincerely think that a movement like ours can communicate this message more easily because we come from the projects and we are living in them now.

During certain debates we encountered aggressive young men who did not understand our arguments, who refused to hear anything about neighborhood violence, and who accused us of stigmatizing the suburbs. During several rallies we faced harsh criticism, and we were violently rejected by some who felt they were under attack. We even met boys who had participated in several collective rapes and who did not understand what was wrong with their behavior and why we were protesting. It was horrifying to see that these young men could not grasp the weight of their acts and how they had destroyed a young woman's life.

I understand that it might be difficult for a boy living in the projects to listen to a rebuke about violence when he constantly experiences feelings of injustice. And thus that some of them move from the status of victim to that of persecutor. Social, cultural, and intellectual poverty as well as macho principles acquired through experience prevent these young men from understanding that they too feel the effects of this system now governing the projects. During the meetings, their anger mounted as they thought that young women had decided to declare war on them. The image of our movement they had retained from the media was one of hostility to men.

We had many discussions with them, either as individuals or as a group. Together with other young women in the march, we tried to explain that the march was not organized against the neighborhoods, neither against our fathers and brothers, nor against Islam, but it was a movement that allowed us to exist as women who deserve respect. We simply wanted to escape the spiraling violence that was destroying everyone in the projects. We wanted them to understand that they were themselves victims but also actors because of their behavior toward young women. We explained that we also had brothers who had been sent to prison because they had skidded out of control or been caught with bars of hash, that our little sisters had been assaulted by boys in the projects. In fact, we were talking about something that we had experienced and that our paths were the same as theirs.

Even though it was sometimes difficult to make ourselves heard, the majority of young men ended up understanding and admitting what we said, when we took the time to show them some consideration and to explain. Afterward some of them, on returning to the projects, began to ask themselves questions and change their behavior toward young women. The girls were the ones who later told us. The seed we had planted began to grow in their minds.

Others, on the contrary, still refuse to support us and exclaim in loud voices that we have "betrayed the community." Our actions do, in fact, upset them. First there are the gang leaders who operate in the parallel economy, because our denunciations have shed light on their activities, their organization, and their trafficking. Opposition next comes from religious leaders among the Muslim fundamentalists who will not hear of women's emancipation. At several stopovers they came to create disorder in our meetings, to insult us as heathens and to threaten us with a fatwa.

Resistance also comes from an association titled Ni Machos Ni Proxos (Neither Machos Nor Pimps), a male collective that started up in spring 2003 in opposition to our movement, denying the reality we have described and denouncing the supposed stigmatization and demonizing we were provoking. But we faced their criticism, we knew that we were right and that we needed to remain steadfast. We also come from the housing projects, and they cannot lie to us about the educational privileges they received, or about the law of the strongest they confirm by maintaining their positions. During our last stopover in Asnières on 6 March 2003, they attended the meeting we organized with the intention of totally sabotaging it. After an hour of sterile debate, during which they gave us to understand that they were not there to listen but to sabotage our work, the leader finally declared that he preferred facing off against Le Pen in the projects in Asnières than against us. Needless to say, he left with his acolytes accompanied by a chorus of booing.

LIBERATING THE NEED TO SPEAK OUT

Our success finally overwhelmed us. At each meeting we realized that the audience before us did not come only from the projects to talk about violence. The audience was very mixed—middle class, teachers, bourgeois from the center of town, and workers from the suburbs—and had wide-ranging expectations. When we began to talk about the violence we experienced, we were thinking about the need for boys and girls in the projects to speak out, but not for society as a whole to be so engaged.

In these debates expectations ran very high, almost more than we could satisfy. People came to discuss the violence in the neighborhoods, but they also questioned us about the economy, about unemployment, about things we could not address. These were matters that political leaders, local authorities should address. After 21 April 2002 and Jean-Marie Le Pen's eligibility for the run-off presidential election, people expressed a huge need to speak out, a need for democracy and an exchange of ideas. I understood that our French citizens were tired of having the debate confiscated by others, that they wanted to talk about their experiences but had not been given a space. Le Pen's score in the presidential election had caused widespread fear. Sometimes the way in which the audience was divided in the meeting halls in certain cities such as Lille or Lyon made us tremble: the whites sat on one side of the room, the blacks and Rebeus on the other. On these evenings I felt that a split had developed in the public and that a debate on the republic, on secularism and the place of Islam was essential.

As a follow-up to the march and to extend our activities, in April 2003 we formed the association Ni Putes Ni Soumises. The idea came to us during the march, for we were often asked about our next steps, what we planned to do after the march so that people could get involved, and so on. We had a huge number of membership requests from individuals, from associations that wanted to create Ni Putes Ni Soumises committees. The demands came from girls and boys from the projects but also from primary school teachers, doctors, and lawyers. Several elected officials, on the Left as well as the Right, and regional administrative councils also contacted us. As we wanted to maintain our independence, we proposed helping them set up committees on the condition that young neighborhood women would run them. This solution worked and the committees now represent the ethnic diversity of the republic I love; they include all ages, social classes, and ethnic origins, blacks, whites, and Rebeus. All of those who marched with us felt great satisfaction in seeing the committees established.

Ni Putes Ni Soumises, which was the slogan of our manifesto in January 2002, now trademarked, has become the name of our new association. But because the name is sometimes difficult for groups in the projects to use, each committee can take the name it wishes. We are linked to these groups by the movement's charter that all must respect.

9

Is Feminism No Longer Relevant?

To understand our relationship to feminism, you have to understand where we come from. Talk about feminism in the projects, about women's struggles, and all the girls burst out laughing. Such references have no meaning for them because the social gains from these movements never entered the projects. The choice of sexuality, the right to contraception and to abortion are "not for them." They are denied access to these rights. This is a bitter statement, but one based on reality.

WHAT FEMINISM MEANS IN THE PROJECTS

When you talk about the pill or contraception to a woman, you assume that she has already begun to be sexually active. Well, any hope for sexual relationships is off-limits for young women in the projects! Virginity is such an obligation that no young woman can calmly admit that she has had sexual relations with a man. It's impossible. You would never hear a girl from the projects say that she takes the pill or that she is by accident pregnant and that she is going to get an abortion. If she acts like a free woman who has a sex life, the men make her pay dearly for it. It is enough that she slept once with a young man from the project—and that people know it—for her to acquire a reputation, to have her brother made fun of because he had not policed his sister, and to set in motion her repression by the family. All the adolescent women in the projects, including women in headscarves, have a love life that includes sex. But it is clandestine; sexual relations are hidden and often take place in sordid circumstances—in cellars, in cars, in cheap hotels—and under deplorable conditions, without protection.

In the projects no young woman would ever claim to be a feminist, except perhaps if she had political training, which would concern only a very small minority today. The word "feminism" is completely hackneyed, outdated, obsolete, even ridiculous in the eyes of many. In the imagination of young women from the projects, to be a feminist means to be against men, to be permanently at war with men, like the Amazons. Among the men and women who participated in the march, no one referred to the feminist liberation movements of the 1970s, not even I. In Clermont-Ferrand I had already taken part in feminist groups, such as Droit de choisir (the right to choose).[1] But I quickly abandoned the

---

1. [Trans.] The organization Amara refers to, Choisir, was founded by the lawyer Gisèle Halimi in the early 1970s to promote the right to contraception and abortion, and to defend women who had signed a manifesto in April 1971 declaring that they had had recourse to abortion (which had been banned by law in 1920). See Claire Duchen, *Feminism in France: From May '68 to Mitterand* (London: Routledge, 1986).

group because we never discussed anything concrete, such as the cases I handled at Solidarity House of young women who had run away from home, cases for which I would have welcomed help. Most of the time these women's groups discussed only feminist theory or globalization. Because their political outlook was not our first priority, my colleagues at Solidarity House and I felt at odds with them. We wanted to be able to respond to the urgent situations of the women who came to our office.

POSSIBLE RAPPROCHEMENT

Yet during the march people soon labeled us "feminists," as if the connection was obvious. We met militants from associations and many individual women whose life experiences strangely resembled our own. Up until then, I had imagined that macho violence was a minority phenomenon in the middle classes. I was convinced that if you had money you could always escape. But in meetings we faced an incredible number of girls and women who came from wealthy families and who related the violence to which they were subjected: conjugal rape, rape of all kinds, beatings by husbands or boyfriends, daily harassment, treatment that made them lose all confidence in themselves. Many confessed that they were speaking out for the first time, thanks to others' testimony. Thus, we had the proof before us of a general regression in the condition of women. These women from wealthy families who came to testify about their suffering opened my eyes to the law of silence about sexual violence that is rife in all social milieus. The projects do not have a monopoly on it, even though the problem is somewhat magnified there.

We were horrified by this discovery, we who assumed that women from the wealthy classes had benefited from the feminist movement's gains. Despite the rhetoric, the adoption of the law on parity, and the image mediated by women's magazines, these women were also in trouble. And so we had to ask ourselves, if wealthy women did not have the means to resolve their problems of violence, would they be able to help us rise above ours? Moreover, we wanted to get out of our catastrophic situation without resorting to arguments of victimization. But we suddenly realized that the struggle was going to be more difficult and longer than we had initially imagined. We felt an immediate solidarity with the women we met. Hence we would no longer simply try to help young women in the projects but rather put our energy into improving the lives of all women.

The words of a student named Myriam quite accurately reflect the shifting opinion of feminism among all the women and girls who marched or who followed our movement:

> At the outset, for me feminism represented a struggle by hysterical and vengeful women. Moreover, I thought it was useless. At that time I believed that if we resolved problems of social inequality, we could at the same time solve women's problems. Therefore feminism was ineffective; it was better to try to advance everyone's rights. Little by little I changed my ideas. Through discussions with other women and in particular with feminists, I understood that women's issues should be considered in their own right. Today, not only do I consider myself a feminist, but I think that this movement can also help resolve social problems.[2]

2. Testimony cited from the *Livre blanc des femmes des quartiers.*

Our new awareness of the generalized and constant oppression of women in French society led us to choose International Women's Day, 8 March, as the arrival date for the march in Paris. I wanted to take advantage of the symbolic meaning of this day to remind others that earlier demonstrations had ignored women's issues. We wanted 8 March 2003 to represent a grand demonstration by women in Paris and by those once-neglected women from the projects—present en masse—because this symbolic day belonged equally to them. By appropriating 8 March for ourselves, for all female immigrant children, including myself, we were demonstrating our desire to be full citizens of French society. In this way we were telling young women in the projects that the issue of women's place in society touched them, that it was part of their lives, and that they had to participate in their own way.

A SPECIAL INTERNATIONAL WOMEN'S DAY

At the outset we worked in isolation. Some feminist associations had already planned a march similar to the ones in previous years and were reluctant to modify it. We had the impression that some feared that we would take over their demonstration. But what we wanted was not to participate in a classic, rather static, demonstration but, on the contrary, to create an event that would be remembered. Then, little by little, as the march met with success at stopovers, several associations and individuals joined up with us; a representative group formed and made the idea of a large demonstration, with our marchers at its head as we arrived in Paris, seem obvious. The labor unions gave us their backing, and we found valuable logistical support from women union leaders at the local and national level. Everyone joined the demonstration in Paris: all the political parties, with the obvious exception of the Far Right; labor unions; feminist movements such as CADAC (coordinated associations for abortion and contraception), GAMS (women's group for the abolition of sexual mutilation), Planning familial (family planning), Femmes contre les inté-grismes (women against fundamentalism), Chiennes de garde, Mix-Cité, and Les Femmes en Noir;[3] but also the photographer Kate Barry and many others. Mohammed Abdi, the secretary-general of the Federation of Solidarity Houses, took time off from work to offer his experience in organizing the day's events and largely contributed to their success by his remarkable work.

In my opinion, the march had mixed results. On the one hand, it was a real victory to see all these people marching behind our banner, Ni Putes Ni Soumises, carried by girls from the projects. We could not count in advance on mobilizing thirty thousand people for a movement like ours! For the eight marchers who started in Vitry-sur-Seine, it was an achievement and a form of recognition for the relevance of our message. Many young people came from the projects to participate, including black and Beur

3. [Trans.] Chiennes de garde (watchdog association) was founded in 1999 to defend women in public office from attacks and from sexist insults and obscenities (the insult most often heard is *pute* [whore]). One of the association's goals is to obtain an antisexist law, similar to the 1972 antidefamation law against racism and anti-Semitism. See its Web site, www.chiennesdegarde.org. • Mix-Cité calls itself a "feminist, anti-sexist and universalist" association to promote gender equality. See www.mix-cite.org. • Les Femmes en Noir, like the Women in Black in Jerusalem, demand the creation of a Palestinian state based on the 1967 borders with the state of Israel. The Paris-based group seeks to bridge the gap between the Jewish and Muslim communities in France. See its Web site, www.lesfemmesennoir.org.

boys and many girls. And for the first time our mothers in their headscarves demonstrated—I thought their presence was extraordinary. They had listened to us and now began to express their demands, although they had never done so before in their lives: this was a real breakthrough. On the other hand, we knew that people from the projects rarely participate in demonstrations and that pulling them in would be hard. But I was a little disappointed that they did not turn out in larger numbers. I would have loved to see the projects flood the streets of Paris. Still, this proved to be only the beginning. Since the march took place, we have often been asked to speak in secondary schools. The debate has continued in homes, as daughters are now speaking to their fathers and mothers. We have restored the dialogue between parents and children, between brothers and sisters and between girlfriends and boyfriends. This was fundamental.

THE RENEWAL OF FEMINIST STRUGGLES

Our strategy today is to engage in the feminist struggles but not to fall back into those small groups reserved for wealthy women. We must also make our voices heard in a strange intellectual debate that divides the feminist milieus. As I understand this debate, the "universalists" are opposed to the partisans of inherent differences. The former conceive of the individual as universal, without sexual distinctions; they consider that differences between men and women are socially constructed; and they believe that the remaining battles for women concern demands for full equality with men. The latter, partisans of inherent difference, assert that there are natural differences between men and women, that women must cope with specific oppression by men, that they live in situations of violence, and that the solution to these problems requires recognition of separate spaces for each sex. But because the worsening of women's situation in France today represents a collective failure, we need to clarify the goals of the feminist movement and, for this purpose, to evaluate past struggles and tactics.

I am equally persuaded that we need to stop thinking of women as victims and referring to the war of the sexes. This formulation was probably useful in the 1970s to get particular results in the battle for equality, but today it is not meaningful. Such ways of seeing the world would start a war in the projects. I think we need to start from concrete situations and preserve the universalist message that men and women are citizens with the same rights. In my opinion, citizenship has no sexual distinction. To be sure, society is composed of men and women, but they are above all citizens of the republic that guarantees their rights. In France, women normally benefit from the gains of feminist movements, and rights exist. Now they need to protect all women, including the young women in the projects. Feminist groups today must understand that, beyond the battle for the respect for women's rights in the constitution and under the law, there are urgent social questions that need to be resolved, and that these are also republican issues.

Sadly, feminist movements have forgotten social questions. In my opinion, the best example of their denial of the question of class is the debate that raged over prostitution. On this very issue, I am not ready to follow the lead of Elisabeth Badinter.[4]

4. [Trans.] A controversial author, Elisabeth Badinter advocates feminism's differentialist strand.

For me, the freedom to prostitute myself is senseless. I only know that my women friends who are prostitutes work only because they are forced to do so for economic reasons, because they need the money to survive and feed their children. Some became prostitutes because they fell in love with their pimp. This is one of the realities of prostitution! I would not consider those who choose this work to be prostitutes, and I do not judge them in any way.

During the past few years feminists have been carrying on a private battle of sorts. By focusing on the struggle for parity, they drew on the middle and upper classes and forgot the women of the popular classes. It is very important that the law in favor of parity was passed, but after so many years of struggle, the results are slim. We need to regroup around essential issues such as the struggle against sexist violence, against conjugal violence, in favor of equal pay, for greater professional mobility. In fact, we need to attack all areas where gender equality is not respected. The notorious glass ceiling still exists for women, even more so for the girls from the projects! We need to remember that a young woman from the suburbs does not have the same opportunities as a woman from the bourgeois sixteenth arrondissement of Paris. For this reason, this universalist combat must be fought by all women and by men as well.

The Battle Ahead

On the day the march arrived in Paris we received a phone call from the prime minister's office extending an invitation by Jean-Pierre Raffarin to meet with the marchers. You can imagine our emotion! The previous day a journalist had asked me whether we hoped for a meeting with the government, and I had remarked facetiously "Why not?" We were exhausted by five weeks of marching and by the pressure that had built up little by little. But it was indeed incredible: we had begun the march in a climate of general indifference and, on arrival, we had been invited to meet the prime minister! The marchers welcomed the news with pride because it meant that our efforts had succeeded and that people were finally listening. For me, it was an encouraging sign.

OUR PROPOSALS TO THE PRIME MINISTER

Thus, several hours before the demonstration in Paris we found ourselves sitting in the salon of the prime minister's residence at

Hôtel Matignon. He was accompanied by François Fillon, the minister of social affairs, Jean-Louis Borloo, the secretary of state for urban policy, and Nicole Ameline, the delegate-minister for gender parity and professional training. We had a frank discussion about what was happening in the projects and we presented our five priority proposals: the preparation of an educational guide on respect for women, written for young people; the urgent creation of shelters for young runaway women; the organization of special reception centers within police stations for victims of male violence; the creation of special neighborhood "listening posts" where women could go for advice; and the launching of a training program by our movement Ni Putes Ni Soumises to educate women organizers for work in the projects. We had the impression that day that our demands were truly heard. An interministerial committee, headed by Nicole Ameline, was established very rapidly after our meeting to carry out our proposals.

On the first proposal, we obtained the government's commitment to issue a guide on respect for women, financed by the prime minister's office, for distribution in September 2003 by the Ministry of Youth and National Education in the projects, but especially in the primary and secondary schools. The administrators of the Paris region showed their support for the follow-up on this project. This guide might appear to be just another gimmick, but it deals with a reality. We believe, in fact, that it is indispensable to bring the message to young men who live in a macho culture that women must be respected, and the sooner they learn this the better. Beyond reminding them of the rules for living in a society based on mutual respect, the guide offers practical advice for how to deal with concrete situations drawn from collected testimony.

On the second proposal, the creation of shelters for young women who have run away from home or who are at risk—offering temporary housing, a kind of halfway house where they could relocate, continue their studies, and live free from daily pressure and violence—Jean-Louis Borloo, the secretary of state for urban policy, promised us about a hundred apartments for fall 2003. But this number will not be sufficient to respond to the requests all over France. Beyond these few apartments we need to create a national structure on a larger scale that would take into account all facets of this problem.

As for the third, a specific reception center inside police stations was set up. When a group of women marchers met with the minister of the interior, Nicolas Sarkhozy, at his request, he was attentive to our idea and undertook to bring psychologists into the police stations, and to train policewomen to meet with victims of sexual harassment and violence in the projects. We explained our vision of the situation, insisting on the fact that the social environment weighs heavily on certain young men. To be sure, a minority chooses to flout the rules of civil society, but the vast majority of young men aspire to live and grow up in a secular republic. Eliminating the violence in the projects also means establishing certain concrete measures to prevent delinquency. Because kids at risk can unfortunately be identified as early as primary school, the measures need to mobilize all those who interact with children: parents, primary schoolteachers, youth workers, and others. Moreover, at this same meeting we alerted the minister of the interior to the desperate situation of some young women, who find themselves in administrative trouble in France once they have been brought as brides from their home country by men who want them to serve as servants. And when these women revolt, the men threaten to divorce them in order to keep them in line, knowing full well that the women risk deportation, and that once back in their country they will be condemned by social opinion. The minister assured us that on this subject he would make sure that his administration applied the appropriate measures to confront this situation, foreseen by a circular issued on 19 December 2002, so that these young women would not become victims on two counts.[1]

On the next, the government also reacted favorably to the creation of "listening posts." These spaces will offer advice and aid for girls and women from the projects by ad hoc staff who can help them set up their own activities. At the moment there are almost no spaces where neighborhood women can organize. And there is a need for meeting places where women and men can exchange ideas. The idea behind this proposal is to allow women to leave their homes, once again to occupy public spaces that have been confiscated by men. As their projects develop, these women could then invite the men to join them so that the men could also participate in the life of the projects. We need to create spaces that reinvent gender relations on the basis of mutual respect. Ten pilot sites have been identified in France for autumn 2003, five in Paris and the Paris region, five in the provinces. These pilot sites will be funded by local municipalities as part of urban policy.

Finally, we proposed the creation of a university or teach-in program for our movement, Ni Putes Ni Soumises, that would

1. The administrative circular requires government prefects to forward such cases of young women, whose legal residence status has been interrupted by divorce or separation, for review by the Commission on Residence Permits.

be open to other associations as well. The project aims to offer young people from the projects the opportunity to participate in reflection and debate on subjects that concern them but for which they have no structured intellectual support: subjects such as secularism, mechanisms of exclusion, discrimination, gender relations, the republic. All of these themes are vitally important to our movement and are relevant to young women's lives in the neighborhoods. A first session will take place from 3 to 5 October 2003. Subsequently, we plan to have specific training programs for young women who would then become organizers within associations, directors of neighborhood organizations, or managers of listening posts. These training courses must be funded by the state. We want these young women to become the privileged spokeswomen in the projects. Our goals are ambitious but possible. Since the march, many professionals have volunteered to collaborate, including some psychologists who called to say that they were willing and ready to help. While waiting to establish our training school for women in the projects, we are setting up two networks—one staffed by psychologists, another by lawyers—for aid to local associations who are already working on young women's cases.

However, our urgent priority now is to be able to shelter young women at risk. For this reason, during our meeting with government representatives we stressed the pressing need to create a national plan for ad hoc shelters. We could not wait for subsidies to be allocated for this work. We had raised high hopes after the march and we wanted the situation in the projects to change now, especially for young women. Certainly we will be very attentive to the concrete follow-up of all the government's promises.

FURTHER ACTION

The movement will receive financial support for the creation of a social fund that will allow us to respond to urgent cases, to take young women who have been threatened or sexually assaulted out of the projects and find them a place to recuperate. Most of the time, when they run away from home they leave everything behind, including money and personal belongings. The funding we are seeking to organize will allow us to offer them material aid, food, clothing, and money for rent. Emancipation begins only when you have a place to lay your head as well as your burdens.

We had planned to hold a big concert in June 2003 to obtain funds for the first women who had come forward to ask for our help—*les insoumises* (rebels)—but we had to cancel our plans because a strike began. We had counted on bringing people in large numbers from the provinces, and the risk of a transportation strike forced us to cancel the concert. We decided to reschedule it for the following spring in 2004. Twenty-one artists who had volunteered to participate in the concert last June will give benefit performances: they include Rita Mitsouko, La Tordue, Aston Villa, Faudel, Enrico Macias, Jean-Jacques Goldman, Marc Lavoine, Nicole Croisille, but also Lââm and Princesse Aniès, so there will be music for all tastes! Michèle Bernier, Eva Darlan, Daniel Prévost, and Charlotte de Turckheim will act as masters of ceremonies.

More recently, we put together an exhibit titled Mariannes d'aujourd'hui—today's Mariannes—in celebration of Bastille Day, on 14 July, our national holiday. The exhibit consisted of a fresco composed of fourteen portraits of young women wearing the red cap or the tricolor cockade, emblems of the French Revolution of 1789. The exhibit covered the facade of the French National Assembly building, the Palais Bourbon, during most of the summer 2003. This exhibit of young women from the projects, several of whom had marched with us, was conceived and executed by Cécile and Liliane, owners of a gallery of contemporary art (Edgar le marchand d'art) that supports the movement. We envisioned the National Assembly, the heart of the republic, as the last stop of our march. Carrying the symbols of liberty, equality, and fraternity, the march demonstrated the republic's diversity and proclaimed our common bond with Marianne, a woman who embodies resistance to all forms of oppression. This exhibit could not have taken place without the support of Jean-Louis Debré, the president of the National Assembly. Thanks to the effectiveness of his staff, the exhibit was a success. We are very proud to be today's Mariannes.

ACTIVE CITIZENSHIP

To take up the challenge we set ourselves, the movement Ni Putes Ni Soumises must remain independent. We are above all a social movement of citizens who refuse the logic of violence and inequality. We are constructive, not polemical. Our movement's autonomy does not mean maintaining political neutrality. The positions we take are commitments to our fellow citizens, and we will never lose sight of our essential mission: the will to make life change in our housing projects, shattering the law of silence and the law of the strongest forever in our neighborhoods, and replacing them with republican values. I will certainly contribute to the immense undertaking that began on 8 March 2003. But to succeed, we must work together, because it is in everyone's interest to rid our society of ghettos. And it is everyone's duty to preserve the common space that the republic provides and that we must share with mutual respect. All the women and men in our movement work toward this goal. Our movement's demands transcend social classes and political divisions, and this fact delights me all the more because the shock resulting from the 21 April presidential election had left behind great bitterness. For all these reasons I do not fear that others might use our movement for their own political ends. As I stated earlier, we remain vigilant to ensure that our proposals yield results—real and constructive measures, not just promises, that will allow us to respond to the hopes we raised among young people.

Epilogue

Reinvest in the Suburbs!

All the men and women in the march continued to invest their energies in the movement after the final demonstration in Paris on 8 March. While exhausted, we had met with such a wave of sympathy that we no longer had any doubts about our actions. Yet during the march itself emotions ran so high at certain moments that, when several girls and young women confessed their distress and their sufferings to us, we relived our own. In fact, one young woman who was participating in the march had to drop out because her emotions overwhelmed her. I well knew that no one would come through the experience unscathed, and I had told our photographer friend Kate Barry about my concern at seeing people too deeply affected. Thanks to her help, the group of marchers were able to benefit from a psychological support service set up by two very skilled professionals. Today the same group of men and women, with the same determination and energy, are at my side to carry on the fight. Between appearances at secondary schools, demands for aid to set up conferences and committees and debates in the projects, and requests from the media and political leaders, we have been working nonstop. We have also made it a point of honor to respond to letters and e-mails that we have received, often late, because we have been overwhelmed. Our energy has been multiplied because of this solidarity. But we are clearheaded enough to know that the battle will be a long one, notably to change attitudes.

The fact that the battle will be long means that we cannot confine it to women's issues alone but must face up to social reality in the projects and the place that French society affords its young people, particularly those of immigrant parents. Over and beyond the question of violence against women in the projects and in French society as a whole, it is time to reflect on the future of the suburbs. We can trace hypermasculinity, the decline of the neighborhoods into ghettos, the despair of an entire generation of young people, and their impression of being rejected by the rest of society back to their roots in the slow but inexorable abandonment of suburban inhabitants by public authorities. The popular neighborhoods, known discreetly as "sensitive" or "at risk," have changed incredibly in twenty years, but so too have their inhabitants.

During my childhood, we all knew that we young people of the neighborhoods had to fight for our rights and for social equality. But we were convinced that we could make a place for ourselves within the republic whose values we touted. And we believed that the combat we had undertaken would benefit those who were to follow, our sisters and brothers. But today, the young people of the popular neighborhoods do not feel the benefits of the gains for which we fought, and they have doubts about the future. When they leave the projects, they experience the condemning gaze of others that puts them in the wrong, while all they are doing is trying to survive and exist. For too many years now young people from the suburbs have come up against the same political demand to integrate French society. But these young people are for the most part French citizens and consider themselves as such. What does integration mean when you are born in France, when you have gone through a school system that preaches the egalitarian values of citizenship? My generation had already found it painful to hear that we had to integrate even after ten, fifteen, or twenty years of presence in France. Such political demands are unbearable for the third generation.

Today's young people feel the injustice more keenly. Even those who succeeded had the impression of being held back by their social origins at one point or another in their career. And young people who believe in republican values, particularly secular values, who are still numerous in the projects, are silent now. That viewpoint is unpopular and difficult to articulate. But I still believe their aspirations are there, ready to emerge, as the march confirmed. However, words no longer suffice. Each of us must assume our responsibilities and support action for change. This is also what it means to be a citizen.

Public authorities too have an important role to play. Beyond the recognition of the problem, they must demonstrate a real political will for change in the projects through concrete measures. During the period when François Mitterand was president, the minister of urban affairs had undertaken a policy in favor of problem neighborhoods. At least the policy had come into existence, even though it was clear that the measures proposed were insufficient. And today, despite all the goodwill, the minister of

urban affairs does not have sufficient means to carry out fundamental reforms. To attack the suburbs' malaise head-on and
strengthen social cohesion assumes breaking up the ghettos,
favoring social and ethnic diversity, and of course requires far
greater means. We also need many more youth workers and
organizers to help with programs to prevent delinquency. Over
the past few years, the number of jobs available for youth workers assigned to these neighborhoods has drastically declined, and
those who are recruited no longer have adequate training for
problem suburbs. Many of these very young men are just out of
school; when they arrive in our neighborhoods, they are horrified by what they find. Many of them fall apart and ask to be
transferred elsewhere—no one ever explained to them the reality of life in these neighborhoods. The training of youth workers
needs to be better adapted to real life in the projects.

But the heart of the problem is that there are not enough
youth workers to tackle the situation of social degradation. By
far the most urgent need is to recruit large numbers of youth
workers for our neighborhoods, because, in addition to behav-
ioral sanctions, we also need measures of prevention. To prevent
violence and delinquency we need the regular presence of youth
workers in the projects—neither mediators nor older brothers,
but real professionals. Just because a young man lives in the projects and knows all the families, he will not necessarily be able to
manage the conflicts and be a suitable mediator. Young people
from the projects require training as youth workers, because this
experience can only heighten their visibility and allow more of
the younger men to identify with them, giving their work greater
depth and overall value. Several years ago, when Michel Dele-
barre was minister of urban planning, he instituted a special

recruitment program for young people from the projects who had failed out of the school system, helping them prepare the competitive exams to become youth workers and reenter the normal school curriculum. Thanks to this special program, many young men and women in the projects finished their studies and accomplished real work in the neighborhoods.

What the projects need, in addition to the reassuring presence of the police, is more educators, more nurses, and more social workers in schools designated as zones of priority education. We also need to create a corps of psychologists with specific training for work in neighborhoods at risk. Violence is also a sign of distress, and as such it needs professional treatment and follow-up, all funded by the state, because families in the projects cannot afford this type of care.

The suburbs require a specific program of massive investment that would reconstruct and open up the housing projects. It is equally urgent to establish specific training programs of affirmative action for young people and for women, such as the one adopted by the Institut des sciences politiques or the one created by Jean-Pierre Chèvenement in the police (based on specific recruitment of suburban young people and children of immigrants). The time has come to break the glass ceiling that stifles any momentum from the suburbs. Life there is still difficult, yet, as we have seen, talented young people grow up in the projects. Let's not forget those who have succeeded in spite of the difficulties, and in all types of occupations. If these young people have managed to benefit from social mobility, how many, on the contrary, have fallen back? It is imperative to end all forms of discriminatory practice today so that, working together, we can win the battle for the republic.

Postscript

I would never have imagined this book would create such a sensation. Through the lens of my personal history and experience, I wanted to convey our critical situation in the suburbs. It is one of exclusion by a disoriented society that lacks confidence in the republic and its values. My objective was to explain why this situation is unbearable, especially for young women, and, quite modestly, to develop some ideas for reflection, to make the notion of "living together" in a secular republic a workable and emotionally rewarding reality.[1]

The public's reception of this book took me by surprise. All the letters and messages of encouragement I received bear witness to this, as do the numerous prizes the book accumulated: prize for the best "political book," a prize for "secularism," for

1. [Trans.] This phrase comes from the Stasi commission's report; Amara was among those interviewed. See the introduction for an analysis of the report in connection with the 2004 law banning the headscarf.

"ethics," for "human rights," and other prizes outside France. Each award was an intense emotional experience, and I felt overwhelmed by the responsibility that would weigh on my shoulders in the future—and on all those who were my daily collaborators in our movement. I rarely found the appropriate words to comment on these distinctions, and so I limited my remarks to simple thanks: the symbol of each prize is powerful and strong. Powerful in the way politics is, because it is noble and essential to democracy. Strong in the way secularism is, because it is our major advantage in the struggle against racism, intolerance, fundamentalism, and sexism. As Jean Rostand said, secularism trains us because "it aims to school minds without conformity, to enrich them without indoctrination, to arm them without force." Hence it prepares us for the shared combat ahead to preserve the notion of living together, and to thwart the retreat into sectarian politics led by the opponents of secularism. Ethics comes next, because without it there would be no civic responsibility and no conviction. And finally, human rights, a combat that marks my life, first as the daughter of immigrant workers, but also and very simply as a woman whose fundamental rights were too often thwarted.

Overwhelming responsibility could never make me forget the magic, joyful meetings with our fellow citizens. Traveling from town to town, I discovered urban and rural France. I saw a country bursting with generosity and energy despite the difficulties and doubts. Over and over, people asked about the resurgence of violence against women, about the problems of women in the suburbs, about immigrant women, about the future of our young people, particularly those in the housing projects. Everyone worried about our collective capacity to resolve the phenomenon of exclusion. Everyone was aware that discriminatory practices inhibited many young people's feelings of sharing republican values, and that strong measures were necessary to win them back to the republic.

How many times have strangers, who quickly became friends, welcomed me, there on the station platform or in front of a meeting hall where a public debate they had organized was to take place? How many association organizers have I met—in places where effort seems futile—who spend their days knitting together social bonds and bringing republican values alive? How many times have I been touched, despite my exhaustion, by an invitation to dinner or a meeting from men and women who have opened their homes to me? All these people warmed my heart, as the singer George Brassens said, "by the fire of their generosity." I was proud to have these men and women participate in our debates, even though they were overcome by events, they had lost control over their children, and they knew that the laws of the projects still governed. They publicly rejected the violence that is destroying numbers of young people, they condemned the presence of fundamentalists and their dangerous rhetoric, and they defended the secular republic while recognizing its dysfunction. The silent majority spoke out, and I guarantee that it had a great deal to say. I had many exchanges with these men and women, both young and old, and they enriched my life. I also learned a great deal that allowed me to adapt my approach during the different debates. Now, one year after founding our movement Ni Putes Ni Soumises, we have received numerous invitations to speak, many of which are from schools, and our staff diligently respond because these human contacts are so enriching.

Over this entire period we have constantly tried to explain and convince people that better understanding of relations between girls and boys and between women and men requires a change in outlook. The diversity of tour encounters and the exchange of ideas lead all of us to forge our opinions. Among all these debates, the most physically challenging and the most intense were those over secularism and religious symbols in school. I discovered that, while we all share secularism, certain political leaders and intellectuals have their own ways of defining it.

Concerning the headscarf question, in this book's first edition I commented on the necessity and the urgency of clarifying the situation. At that time I was skeptical of the effectiveness of a law, and I even thought it might stigmatize and create confusion. But now, looking back over all my encounters in France, I realize that this law was more than necessary, and that it was even much anticipated. Even so, the struggle by young women in headscarves requires closer consideration. Personally, I believe the headscarf is nothing more than a means of oppression emanating from a patriarchal society. Yet, paradoxically, for these young women the headscarf is a means of existing within the family that allows them to appropriate the religious discourse that had previously been reserved for men. It also helps them exist in the public space of the projects without the fear of being singled out by certain young men or, very simply, of damaging their reputation. But this immediate and obvious gain is nothing but an illusion of false freedom.

I remain convinced that a number of these young women, who will go as far as they can wearing a headscarf, will become conscious of the ideological confinement it represents. I dare to hope that out of this realization will come a real process of emancipation. Taking a more optimistic outlook, let us wager that, once free of it, they will join the feminist avant-garde. I want to believe in my scenario, but this is also the challenge before us. Progress will not be easy or swift, even if we know that some fundamentalist organizations, by supporting the right of young women to wear the headscarf in school, offer them only social death as a future.

Our republican tour de France that took place from early February to 8 March 2003 definitely confirmed the positions we had taken. The debate on the Stasi commission's report on secularism was in full swing. Our march had involved us in debates in some thirty towns in France. Working as a team, ignoring difficulties and restrictions, members of our national office and new volunteers who were eager to share their republican ideals carried out the tasks. Thanks to the sponsorship by the French National Railroads and by the Accor Company, thanks to the support committees of Ni Putes Ni Soumises and other associations that joined our effort, I can say, with hindsight and objectivity, that our republican tour de France was a great success. I am still amazed by the wonderful organizing skills of our team members under urgent pressure for an event that should have had six months of preparation. Today, I salute their courage and determination. When a problem arose—and this was the case at several times—everyone joined together to find a rapid solution, in the same way as they joined together "to shield me from details that would have bothered me," as they told me so kindly afterward.

This unique experience had the beneficial effect of bonding the team and of creating conditions for unfailing solidarity without sectarianism. Many of the boys and girls, who had never been militants, showed themselves through this adventure to be so capable that they became the core organizers of the march. Some of them worked in the logistical team alongside Sihem, Mala,

Samira, Dalila, Yann, Chantal, Otman, Cécilien, Shéra and Isabelle, while others networked directly with local structures, working under the demanding direction of Safia, assisted by Zorha, Farida, Aïcha, Mustapha, Nordine, Clotilde, Asma, François, and Thierry. And then there was Nora, thanks to whom Franck could spare time for the contacts with the media and other tasks as well. The latter collaborators were a great solace to me through their freshness and energy. They became the spearhead of the movement. They were always accessible and there when needed, together with our friend, the indispensable Slimane, the man who settled everything. He could handle by himself all those details that resembled the proverbial "last straw," absorbing them and calming everyone in moments of tension! Everyone had their assigned tasks, everyone was conscious that "people were waiting for us to make a mistake": we could not afford a false note. Everyone had their score, and like a rigorous and demanding orchestra conductor, Mohammed Abdi, the association's secretary-general, led the movement.

Thanks to the support of the nearly fifty committees established throughout France that form part of our association, and the many willing hands they include, our tour de France was very successful. It was a stunning example of youthful energy in favor of a noble cause: secularism, emancipation, and multiculturalism in our republican melting pot!

At each stopover, together with the young men and women who accompanied me, we met with the local committee, with other associations, and with locally elected officials. In the early evening a public meeting was held that never mobilized less than four hundred people. A crowd of this size confirms that secularism, emancipation, and equal rights remain values that have strong support. It is true that a national debate has revealed a social divide that transcends political leaders and ideological currents. There is a majority that is conscious of the difficulties and problems and remains committed to republican values and to the notion of "living together." There is also an activist minority that operates within a circle of leftists and Islamists (fundamentalists) and tries to explain that the republic is an illusion and capable only of stigmatizing and excluding. Making citizens feel guilty is a nice tactic. This minority was in the audience at all our public debates.

Its presence leads me to believe that orders went out to follow our trail, "those angry females, accompanied by male types who are token members of a false cause," according to what I heard in Lyon. Because I am strongly attached to the democratic process, it was important to me that each woman and man in the audience have the opportunity to speak. I remained vigilant, therefore, that the possibilities for debate were respected. But wherever we went, the activist minority tried by all possible means to take over the debate. I had not foreseen that its members would use threats and pressure to try to silence the majority loyal to the secular republic.

Some of them went to the point of insulting me and several other female leaders of the march who had the courage to participate in the debates. Others accused me of espousing neocolonialism, of betraying my own community origins—showing their real intentions—and of mistreating Islam, thus conflating Islam and Islamism (fundamentalism) in a vicious and shameful way. I was surprised, however, to discover that those who thought they were dealing a death blow, even well-known intellectuals among them, are not the children of immigrants. And several of them had heard about the social problems in the projects only from broadcasts on the evening televised news programs. These same individuals were silent when the majority of the young women from the housing projects were fighting, and are still fighting, to resist pressures from the neighborhood. These same people accuse supporters of the headscarf law of being racist and Islam-haters. For them, the headscarf is only a detail, buried in a list of global demands against a failing system. From their viewpoint, how could anyone dare to punish the victims who wear headscarves when France today refuses to face and assume responsibility for its colonial past, even its colonial present! How absurd, even ridiculous! Islamists use similar arguments in the housing projects to accredit their own rhetoric. As they say, they are obviously right, since even some intellectuals recognize the same truths.

Bravo to these defenders of freedom: when you talk to them about social equality, they agree; when you talk to them about exclusion, they say we must fight against it; but when you talk to them about secularism, they stumble because they lack the courage to follow their reasoning to a logical conclusion. Their thinking is nothing more than a recasting of the tenets of secularism. They have never believed in it as a means of emancipation. They dare not affirm it loud and clear because they know that they will be attacked by our citizens at election time. They employ other methods to impose their viewpoints. As the fundamentalist Islamists do, they flatter those who are susceptible to their discourse. A portion of the new generation can find favor with them, but only by agreeing to wallow in the status of victim, a position that has served them for years. Carried to absurdity, it justifies all forms of violence carried out by victims, because victims cannot be seen as perpetrators of violence. The more learned of these standard-bearers of the ideology of victimization believe that the growing Islamism we have noted is only the expression of a break with the system. For this reason, these intellectuals are convinced that the "revolutionary" energies behind this minority deserve their support. Strange reasoning that requires its proponents to be blind and deaf, in light of the ravages of Islamism today, primarily in Muslim countries and especially against women. The feminist movements in these countries and in others have alerted us to their oppression.

On the pretext of advocating cultural relativism and, therefore, the respect of cultures and traditions (even if the latter diminish personal physical and moral integrity), these manipulators think and speak for others. Observing them and listening to them only confirm my doubts about their misalliance with political Islam. Their cultural relativist mode of thinking was already unacceptable when it advocated tolerance of polygamy, excision, and sexual inequality; it is all the more so in its use of Islam for political ends.

And it is clear for me today that the headscarf represents the political symbol that we must fight at all costs if we want to avoid falling back into obscurantism. All of the rhetoric professed by the activist minority just described is only hypocrisy and lies. It aims at co-opting a number of young people for political and electoral reasons and seriously infringes on the struggle against racism.

In this same spirit, it urges the refusal to march against anti-Semitism under the pretext that such a demonstration would have to be opened up to protests against all forms of racism. Those who hold such positions have a short and selective memory. They would like the general public to believe that the children of Arab-Berber-Muslim immigrants do not worry about anti-Semitism, as if this struggle concerned only Jews, whereas the combat against other forms of discrimination concerned other groups, and them in particular. Thus they co-opt the struggle for human rights as "ethnic," close ranks, and build their reputation on identity politics as the spokesmen in particular for Muslims. I want it to be known that I support the combat against anti-Semitism and the struggle against all other infringements of human rights, much like thousands of others, young women and men like me. Anti-Semitism represents a special page of our history, the drama of the Shoah still resonates in our collective memory and it is a crime to try to diminish the impact it must continue to have on our young people, so that together we can proclaim "No, never again!"

Today's events remind us of certain periods when we failed in our duties, so that we would not be speaking of racism and discrimination today if we had been more vigilant. Past forms of anti-Semitism take on a new life in unexpected ways in certain housing projects. Islamists are constructing an anti-Semitic ideology and justify the horror by using the Israeli-Palestinian conflict and by refusing to come out clearly in support of the appeals to demonstrate against this hydra of hate.

What has happened to all the slogans of the past, ones such as "Première, deuxième, troisième génération, nous sommes tous des enfants d'immigrés" (First, second, third generation, we are all children of immigrants")? By an extraordinary conjuring trick, no one refers any longer to immigration or immigrants, but only to "Muslims." We encountered divisive tactics of this kind during the 2004 demonstration for International Women's Day. For continuity with the great national debate, we had particularly hoped to assemble feminist associations of all tendencies, together with political and labor organizations, on a platform of progressive values such as secularism, equality, and the mixing of class and sex. It did not happen. We received an appeal to participate in the demonstration that listed a hodgepodge of groups, thrown together by circumstances and political expediency. Others pressured us to accept it, but we could not, and instead sent out our appeal, signed by several other feminist, antiracist, and secular organizations as well. And on 8 March the lineup for the demonstration reflected the disparity: our movement Ni Putes Ni Soumises followed the group from CADAC (working for abortion and contraception), while the procession of women in headscarves marched at the end. The serious shortcomings of this historic event—for which young women in the projects had such high expectations—left an indelible mark.

But divisive tactics and pressures did not mislead anyone, and many people came to march with us. I was extremely proud to march alongside political and association leaders. The presence of Nicole Guedj and Madame Arlette Laguiller from Lutte ouvrière was a sign of a real rally around fundamental values. Since that date, insults and abuse have been hurled against members of our movement. Far from discouraging us, such treatment has reinforced our determination to continue.

Because women's struggle is universal and solidarity is international, the movement's message has crossed our borders. Fifty committees on French territory, including one in Nouméa in New Caledonia, and others in Europe and elsewhere strengthen the movement. We have received invitations to exchange ideas with women's groups from Germany to Belgium, from Spain to Italy, from Portugal to England. Dynamic support has also come from the North African countries of Morocco, Tunisia, and Algeria, along with Burkina Faso, Mali, and Senegal. At a greater distance, the United States and Canada each sent us a delegation, and I visited Canada. There are high expectations. Thanks to such reactions from women across the world, we have envisioned organizing an international women's meeting in Madrid sometime in the near future.

Because the struggle for women's emancipation has become the epicenter of the combat against obscurantism and fundamentalism, we can be proud of the progress we have made since the March by Neighborhood Women for Equality and against the Ghetto. Since the death of Sohane, many of us have become conscious of the injustice that affected much of our population. Thanks to the mobilization of public opinion, we have been able to help many young women who were totally alienated. From the exhibit of the Mariannes d'aujourd'hui on the facade of the National Assembly in Paris on 14 July 2003 to our movement's first teach-in in 2004, we carry on our unrelenting combat to preserve secularism, equality, and a plurality of social identities in a multicultural republic.

Fate has taken Samira Bellil, our sister, our friend, our shooting star (as her mother, Nadia, called her). I cannot find the words to speak of her. She was radiant and generous. She was a woman we will miss forever. Proud and rebellious, she lives in the memory of all women and of everyone. Her strength will guide us.

Fadela Amara, president of the
movement Ni Putes Ni Soumises
September 2004

A NATIONAL APPEAL FROM NEIGHBORHOOD WOMEN

Ni Putes Ni Soumises! (March 2002)

We women, who are living in suburban neighborhoods and who come from many origins and faiths, believers and nonbelievers, appeal for our rights to liberty and to emancipation. We are socially oppressed by a society that confines us in ghettos that have become sites of poverty and exclusion.

We are crushed by the machismo of our neighborhood men, who in the name of "tradition" deny our most fundamental rights.

Meeting here for the first Estates General of Neighborhood Women, we affirm our will to win our rights, our freedom, our femininity. We refuse to be forced to make false choices, to be bound by tradition, or to sell our bodies to a commodity society.

No more lessons of morality: our condition as women has been degraded. Political leaders and the media have done little or nothing to help us.

No more sordid realism. We have had enough of others speaking for us and being treated with scorn.

No more justifications of our oppression in the name of the right to difference and of respect for those who force us to bow our heads.

No more silence during public debates over the violence, the precariousness, and the discrimination.

The feminist movement has deserted our neighborhoods. In urgency, we have decided to act.

For us the struggle against racism and exclusion, and the battle for our freedom and emancipation, are one and the same struggle. We alone can free ourselves from this double oppression.

We are speaking out in this appeal in order that our sisters and our mothers in each housing project in France may hear this call to freedom and join our struggle for a better life in our neighborhoods.

So that we may be heard, distribute this appeal as widely as possible, and join us in all the feminist and antiracist initiatives that are the focus of our struggle!

THE MANIFESTO
OF NEIGHBORHOOD WOMEN

Ni Putes Ni Soumises, now and on our terms
(April 2002)

When men suffer, women bear their suffering. Economic marginalization and discrimination have built suburban ghettos where male citizens feel the loss of equality and female citizens even more so. We are the neighborhood women who have decided to shatter the silence concerning the injustice we experience, and who refuse to be forced into submission in the name of "tradition" and of "religion" or simply of violence.

Life in our neighborhoods, for the families who live here, for our children and their future, will not progress if we as women do not regain our place and our dignity.

We denounce the omnipresent sexism, the verbal and physical violence, the forbidden sexuality, the gang rape, the forced marriages, the brothers who become the guardians of the family honor or the police of the neighborhoods. By denouncing all this we refuse the logic of the ghetto that would confine all of us in violence if we did not revolt.

At this moment, when everyone seeks a solution to the violence that undermines our society, we affirm that the first step must be our liberation and the respect of our most basic rights. Public authorities, the media, and political parties speak about the suburbs solely in masculine terms.

As women we appear in public from time to time as docile, doing well in school or in the kitchen preparing meals for the neighborhood festival. Silence covers our lives, silence about the young women who run away, those who do the housework from morning to night, those who conceal themselves in order to love, or those who become mothers in early adolescence.

So we have decided not to wait until things go from bad to worse, but to act in order to change our lives and those of our families in the neighborhoods. Some people may find it unacceptable that we are speaking out, breaking taboos about things that are hidden from others. To those who feel this way, we say: how can you overcome injustice, racism, failure in school, banishment, and imprisonment, if you oppress us women as well?

Millions of women in the suburbs refuse the false choice between submitting to ghetto violence and selling their bodies for survival. We are neither whores nor submissives, simply women who want to live in freedom in order to bring about our desire for justice.

Here is a list of our demands.

The institution of a state policy to strengthen republican values and to promote social peace—the creation of structures that would ensure access to basic rights:

- The right to sex education for all
    Knowledge of the body
    Modes of contraception
    Information on sexually transmitted diseases
- The right to civic education
    Advanced language training
    Courses on civic education
    Legal counseling by trained professionals
    Knowledge of civil rights
    Access to information, guidance, and, if necessary, assistance on
        demand
- The right to safety and security for all
    Specific counseling hours for victims of sexual harassment

Creation of emergency shelters for victims—of moral and physical violence (couples or others), or of forced marriage and polygamy

Creation of counseling centers within police stations in touch with structured programs of aid to women

Creation of a legal structure allowing French consular services abroad to protect and repatriate French citizens or foreigners living in France who were forced into marriage

Measures to combat sources of prostitution (polygamy, clandestine networks, family separation, etc.)

- Recognition of associations—and particularly neighborhood women's associations—as equal partners in local participative democracy

    Specific and follow-up funding for these associations' different activities and for training women in leadership

    Provision of meeting rooms for practical training in local democracy

- Urban policy in favor of mixed-sex activities

    Creation of mixed-sex projects

    Promotion of action for effective access to culture and leisure

    Better recognition and representation of neighborhood women's associations in different state structures at the community level

    Promotion of initiatives to create links between city centers and suburbs

- Programs for families to relieve the daily constraints on women

    New child-care centers

    Measures to reduce the costs for child-care centers

    Better provision of child care on demand

- Creation of a voluntary job program

    Provisions for job stability

    Reinforcement of existing measures and stringent application of the anti-discrimination law

    Strict application of laws for professional equality

- Creation of a mixed-sex and democratic educational policy

    Sustained advocacy of the French melting-pot policy, and of mixed-sex schools

Enhanced guidelines for vocational orientation

Provisions for attractive and accessible career tracks currently
reserved for young men

Abolishment of dead-end career tracks that lead to unskilled jobs
(or unemployment)

BIBLIOGRAPHY
AND FURTHER READING

Balibar, Etienne. "Dissonances within *laïcité*." *Constellations* 11 (2004): 353–67.

Bellil, Samira. *Dans l'enfer des tournantes*. Paris: Denoël, 2005.

Blanc-Chaléard, Marie-Claude. *Histoire de l'immigration*. Paris: La Découverte, 2001.

Bourdieu, Pierre, and Abdelmalek Sayad. *Le déracinement, la crise de l'agriculture traditionnelle en Algérie*. Paris: Editions de Minuit, 1964.

Bouzid. *La Marche*. Paris: Sindbad, 1984.

Chebel, Malek. *L'esprit de sérail: mythes et pratiques sexuels au Maghreb*. 2nd ed. Paris: Editions Payot et Rivages, 2003.

Derderian, Richard L. *North Africans in Contemporary France: Becoming Visible*. New York: Palgrave Macmillan, 2004.

De Wenden, Catherine Wihtol, and Rémy Leveau. *La Beurgeoisie: les trois âges de la vie associative issue de l'immigration*. Paris: CNRS Editions, 2001.

Duchen, Claire. *Feminism in France: From May '68 to Mitterand*. London: Routledge, 1986.

Feldblum, Miriam. *Reconstructing Citizenship: The Politics of Nationality Reform and Immigration in Contemporary France*. Albany: State University of New York Press, 1999.

Freedman, Jane, and Carrie Tarr, ed. *Women, Immigration and Identities in France*. New York: Berg, 2000.

Gaspard, Françoise, and Farhad Khosrokhavar. *Le foulard et la République*. Paris: La Découverte, 1995.

Gillette, Alain, and Abdelmalek Sayad. *L'immigration algérienne en France*. 2nd ed. Paris: Entente, 1984.

Helvig, Jean-Michel, ed. *La laïcité dévoilée*. Paris: Libération et Editions de l'Aube, 2004.

Noiriel, Gérard. *The French Melting Pot*. Translated by Geoffroy de Laforcade. Minneapolis: University of Minnesota Press, 1996.

Sayad, Abdelmalek. "Les trois 'âges' de l'immigration algérienne." *Actes de la recherche en sciences sociales* 15 (1977).

Stora, Benjamin. *Algeria, 1830–2000: A Short History*. Translated by Jane Marie Todd. Ithaca: Cornell University Press, 2001.

———. *La gangrène et l'oubli: la mémoire de la guerre d'Algérie*. Paris: La Découverte, 1991.

———. *Ils venaient d'Algérie: l'immigration algérienne en France 1912–1992*. Paris: La Découverte, 1992.

———. *Le transfert d'une mémoire: de "l'Algérie française" au racisme anti-arabe*. Paris: La Découverte, 1999.

Weil, Patrick. *La France et ses étrangers*. Paris: Calmann-Lévy, 1991.

———. *Qu'est-ce qu'un Français?* Paris: Grasset, 2002.

www.niputesnisoumises.com

INDEX

Abdi, Mohammed, 58, 133, 156
abortion rights, 128, 129n
Accor Company, 116, 155
AIDS education, 77
Alaoui, Fouad, 22
Algerian immigrants: associations of, in 1980s, 14–15; Beur movement of, 12–13, 29nn15,17; citizenship status of, 8–9, 49; during colonial period, 5; emigration of, to France, 6–7, 9–10, 28nn6,8; housing projects of, 47–48; political response to, in 1980s, 10–11; as share of foreign population, 29n12; state welfare provisions for, 10. *See also* Muslim community; Muslim young men; Muslim young women
Algerian War, 7–8, 28nn9,10, 58
Amara, Fadela: on anti-Semitism, 159–60; on Beur movement, 55–56; book awards to, 4, 151–52; on childhood experiences, 48–50; on citizenship, 135; criticism of, 3, 16, 18, 123–25; ethnic background of, 1, 47; at Federation of Solidarity Houses, 108–9; on headscarves, 19, 74–75, 99–101, 154–55; housing project of, 47–48; on International Women's Day, 2004, 160–61; on march's achievements, 133–34, 152–53; on march's participants, 155–56; militant beginnings of, 15, 55–59; mother's encouragement of, 120–21; movement founded by, 2–3; on movement's internationalization, 161–62; patriarchal upbringing of, 44–46, 67–68; on police injustice, 13, 51, 53–54; regional identity of, 43–44; on schooling, 49, 50–52; on second-generation freedoms, 59–60, 83;

Text: 10/15 Janson

Display: Janson

Compositor: International Typesetting and Composition

Indexer: Patricia Deminna

Cartographer: Bill Nelson

Printer and binder: Maple-Vail Manufacturing Group

understand ways feminisms manafests among women in the 21st century (FR & Africa)